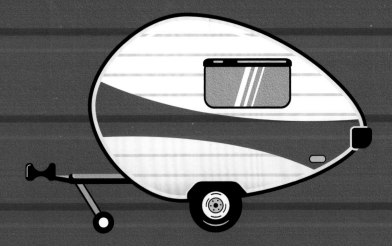

D1343906

I2812331

Brimming with creative inspiration, how-to projects, and useful information to enrich your everyday life, Quarto Knows is a favorite destination for those pursuing their interests and passions. Visit our site and dig deeper with our books into your area of interest: Quarto Creates, Quarto Cooks, Quarto Homes, Quarto Lives, Quarto Drives, Quarto Explores, Quarto Gifts, or Quarto Kids.

© 2017 Quarto Publishing Group USA Inc.

First published in 2017 by Cool Springs Press, an imprint of The Quarto Group, 401 Second Avenue North, Suite 310, Minneapolis, MN 55401 USA. T (612) 344-8100 F (612) 344-8692 www.QuartoKnows.com

Cool Springs Press titles are also available at discount for retail, wholesale, promotional, and bulk purchase. For details, contact the Special Sales Manager by email at specialsales@quarto.com or by mail at The Quarto Group, Attn: Special Sales Manager, 401 Second Avenue North, Suite 310, Minneapolis, MN 55401 USA.

10 9 8 7 6 5 4 3 2 1

ISBN: 978-0-7603-5352-3

Library of Congress Cataloging-in-Publication Data

Names: Peterson, Chris, 1961- author.
Title: Camper rehab : a guide to buying, repairing, and upgrading your travel trailer / Chris Peterson.
Description: Minneapolis, MN, USA : Cool Springs Press, 2017. | Includes index.
Identifiers: LCCN 2017029661 | ISBN 9780760353523 (paperback)
Subjects: LCSH: Travel trailers.
Classification: LCC TL297 .P48 2017 | DDC 629.28/76--dc23
LC record available at https://lccn.loc.gov/2017029661

Acquiring Editor: Madeleine Vasaly
Project Manager: Alyssa Lochner
Art Director: James Kegley
Cover Designer: Kim Winscher
Layout: Kim Winscher
Illustrations: Jeremy Kramer
Photography: Rich Fleischman
Photo Assistance: Georgiy Vyrlan
                 Denis Vyrlan

Printed in China

CAMPER REHAB

A GUIDE TO BUYING, REPAIRING, AND UPGRADING YOUR TRAVEL TRAILER

CHRIS PETERSON

COOL
SPRINGS
PRESS

CONTENTS

INTRODUCTION

Before World War II, camping was a pretty basic affair. You lugged a ridiculously heavy sleeping bag (and maybe an equally ridiculously heavy tent) along in your incredibly uncomfortable backpack. You found a place in the forest that was hopefully not frequented by hungry wild animals. You laid out all your kit, which took about half a day to unpack from that incredibly uncomfortable backpack. You cooked up some not-so-great-tasting food and then, after admiring the stars for a while, climbed into that ridiculously heavy sleeping bag only to find you had apparently laid it on a bed of the pointiest rocks to be found inside a hundred miles.

Camping at this point in history was, understandably, only for the fairly rugged of mind, body, and spirit. Everyone else just stayed home and admired the stars from their backyards or porch swings.

But in the late 1940s, all that changed for the better. In the economic postwar boom, as Americans found themselves with more and more leisure time, and manufacturers found themselves wanting to cash in on that leisure time, along came the reinvention of camping. More precisely, manufacturers refined the camper trailer.

Before actual camper trailers were widely available, the only option for having the comforts of home on a camping adventure was bringing them all with you—including the outhouses.

The iconic Airstream got its start as a small, art deco–influenced tow-behind trailer, shown here with founder Wally Byam. *Courtesy of Airstream Inc.*

Suddenly, that purest of American icons—the open-road, V-8-powered, four-door, boatlike sedan—had a partner. It was a simple tow-behind structure with its own set of wheels and its own identity: a living room for the road. It wasn't a brand-new idea; enterprising individuals had toyed with producing tow-behind "camping trailers" from the 1920s onward. But those early models were basically oversized picnic baskets or tents with wheels. The modern camper trailer was so much more—a way to take convenience and comfort with you into the heart of untamed nature.

These newfangled camping quarters started small, to be sure, the first of them being no more than a galley kitchen and a tiny sleeping space sandwiched between a curved top and a plywood base over a two-wheeled suspension. But the idea caught fire, and campers expanded to answer their growing popularity. Soon enough, they included full-blown, self-contained living quarters with sleeping space for four, dinettes, working stoves, refrigerators, and even—that comfort of comforts among outdoor adventurists—bathrooms!

Suddenly, you could go camping without roughing it. If you were being swarmed by mosquitoes or threatened by bears and mountain lions, you could retreat behind the safety of solid walls. Instead of waiting hours to pull a slimy undersized fish out of an ice-cold river, just so you could half-cook it over your dying fire and spit the bones out between bites of flesh, you could bring your own favorite foods and prepare them however you liked. If it got too cold, or too hot, or too scary to be outside, you could go *inside*. Inside in the great outdoors: what could be better?

THE GOOD OLD DAYS VERSUS MODERN CONVENIENCES

The earliest camper trailers were crafted from materials widely available in the postwar period, including aircraft aluminum, wood, and sheet metal. These materials gave the campers unique appearances and became signature styles for some companies. Airstream, for instance, continues to clad their distinctive rounded camper trailers in polished aircraft aluminum—a cool retro look that has been associated with the company for more than sixty years.

Modern campers are more likely to be wrapped in smooth fiberglass or corrugated aluminum panels. As campers became big business, the camper trailers themselves became more bland, if more comfortable. Manufacturers these days maintain a love affair with the neutral end of the palette, producing interiors in uninspired earth tones full of plastic surfaces with little to distinguish one model from the next.

RIGHT: Many glamping enthusiasts pair vintage cars with older trailers, restoring both. It's not just a pairing of historical accuracy; old-fashioned powerhouse V-8 engines are ideal for pulling trailers of just about any size.

BELOW: Not all retro camper trailers are old. CH Campers is one of a handful of manufacturers producing brand-new retro-styled units. Their "canned ham" trailers capture all the panache of yesterday's finest, with modern conveniences and materials. *Courtesy CH Camper Company*

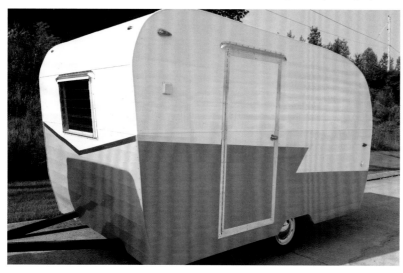

Glamping isn't just about retro style, it's also a way of life that captures the sheer fun of looking back and enjoying the outdoors with flair.

So the question is, what to do when you want the style and originality of a retro model but the conveniences of modern systems and technology? The answer is simple: rehab your own camper. Older campers contain their own "cool" just waiting to be brought back to life, and whether you choose to restore one to its original glory (turquoise, anyone?) or create a totally new vision, they offer a clean slate—usually at a bargain price. They come in funky shapes, with interesting features like jalousie windows that are a rarity in today's streamlined models. They stand out for all the right reasons.

They also offer good value for money. As new camper trailers have come to be equipped with convenience feature on top of convenience feature, the prices have shot up. But if you're willing to forego that stock DVD system or that questionable proprietary undercoating, you just might wind up with the coolest getaway in the neighborhood.

The fact is, most of the conveniences you'll find in today's camper trailers can be retrofit into yesterday's more distinctive, stylish, funky, and fun models. Campers from the 1950s through the early 1980s are finding new life with aftermarket air conditioning, solar panels, microwaves, and satellite internet—all without sacrificing the integral retro flair and charm that are such a draw.

THE GLAMPING MOVEMENT

The idea of combining the thrill of the outdoors with the comforts of home has gone upscale in recent years with the advent of glamping. If you didn't already know, you can probably guess that this is a cross between glamour and camping. Glampers are increasing in number across the country, and that's because glamping combines the practical aspects of camper trailer life and travel with the sheer fun and panache of tooling around in your own customized caravan. Some people even tow their glampers with vintage Cadillacs or classic pickup trucks. Whatever the case, glamping is all about having tons of fun outdoors and looking great doing it.

So the question really isn't whether or not you might want to consider rehabbing an older camper trailer, but more, "Why wouldn't you?" Whether you're creating a truly decked-out conveyance for glamping, letting your creativity run wild with fun design options, or just bringing an older travel trailer back to life with some new conveniences, the draw is the same: fun and comfortable outdoor adventures at an affordable price.

With used campers widely available in just about every price range, it's pretty much guaranteed that there is one out there perfect for your needs and preferences just waiting in the marketplace. And once you latch on to that two-wheeled (or no-wheeled) beauty? You'll have all the advice you need to turn it into your own camping palace or standout glamper paradise in the chapters that follow.

But first things first.

Let's start with the sizes and types of camper trailers available on the used marketplace. You'll want to pick the one that best suits how you intend to camp, and ticks off your checklist of "must-haves."

Any camper renovation or rehab entails deciding to stick with the original look, updating, or creating a hybrid style. Here, the upscale art deco interior perfectly fits with a 1930s Airstream look and feel.

CAMPER TYPES

If you're new to the glamping craze, or if you're only familiar with the kind of camper your mom or grandpa happened to own, you'll soon discover a dizzying array of vintage trailer types from which to choose. Although they range from small and incredibly simple to large and completely outfitted, the camper trailer that's perfect for you usually hinges on two factors: your budget and the type of camping you want to do.

If your budget is a bit tight and you're only looking to take day trips to the beach or the occasional overnight trip to campgrounds that feature their own bathrooms, something like a teardrop or small pop-up might serve you well. On the other hand, if money is no object and you want to basically take a studio apartment with you on your various outdoor adventures, then a full-scale conventional travel trailer with a bathroom, complete kitchen, and luxurious sleeping quarters may be just the ticket. Here's a look at the range of styles you're likely to find in perusing Craigslist or any of the many online trailer classifieds.

TEARDROP TRAILER

PROS
Aerodynamic
Doesn't require a large vehicle
Stylish

CONS
No bathroom
Cramped interior

TEARDROP TRAILER. The most compact and lightweight travel trailer, the teardrop—whose name, quite simply, describes its shape—is a classic, sexy, aerodynamic style. Its key advantages are that it can be towed by a smaller vehicle (no pickup truck required), driving with it is much easier than navigating the road with other styles, and it can cost much less than a larger type. Teardrops usually have a main "cubby" sleeping area—which on taller units doubles as a cramped sitting space—and a small galley kitchen in the back. They are best if you plan on finding campsites with facilities, as this type of camper normally doesn't

Because their small sizes are relatively easy to fabricate, teardrop campers are sided in aluminum, fiberglass, and—as shown here—plywood.

Pop-ups can expand to provide enough room to make a family of four comfortable, and often include amenities such as a full kitchen and a toilet-shower combo.

include a bathroom. Customizing options for teardrops can include painting or decorating the outside and updating the galley kitchen. The sleeping quarters are so small that updating the space pretty much begins and ends at painting the outside, adding nicer upholstery, and introducing new sheets.

POP-UP. Also known as folding camping trailers, these models range from the tiny versions that look almost like suitcases on wheels to more modern A-frame shapes with solid-wall expansion sections. Some expand to a size almost as large as more conventional solid-sided travel campers. The big draw is that when folded up, pop-up trailers are lightweight and don't block the driver's rear view. As an added bonus, some vintage versions feature funky detailing, such as fins and flared wheelwells. By and large, though, the styling is minimal and function trumps form in pop-ups. They can be surprisingly well outfitted. Many include bathrooms, refrigerators, and cooktops. Great for day trips, if you're planning on long-term outings with weeklong campsite stays, a pop-up may be a bit spare and short on comfort.

POP-UP TRAILER

PROS
Lightweight
Lots of features despite small size
Doesn't require a large vehicle
Doesn't obstruct towing vehicle's rear view

CONS
Cramped interior

Truck campers are a way to have much of the luxury of a camper with the driving ease of a pickup truck. You can also take a truck camper—especially one on the back of a four-wheel-drive truck—to remote and difficult-to access-places no towed camper trailer could go.

TRUCK CAMPER. These nifty units are often called "cabover campers" because a sleeping section usually projects out over the cab of the pickup truck, so that the camper can nest in the truck's bed. This is perhaps the easiest camper to drive with. Once settled in the truck bed, it's not a simple job to remove, and most stay in the truck during even long camping trips. Although older versions are simple, with limited space, many truck campers include small cartridge toilets, extendable slide rooms, tops that can be raised and lowered, and many of the features—such as fully equipped galley kitchens—usually associated with full-fledged tow-behind camper trailers.

TRUCK CAMPER

PROS
Larger sleeping area
More feature options than smaller units

CONS
Can't be removed quickly
Requires pickup truck

TRAVEL TRAILER. This is the most popular type of camper trailer on the road and was originally billed as the "tow-behind." That's because the category includes everything from small units that can be towed by a midsize sedan to large luxurious campers that are pulled by pickup trucks or large SUVs. In either case, the tow-behind can be unhitched from the vehicle and stabilized with telescoping jacks, allowing the trailer to be standalone living quarters so that the car or truck can be easily used as convenient local transportation. Be aware that towing a longer travel trailer (anything over 16 feet) can be a draining physical experience, especially if you're driving long distances; the trailer is prone to sway and can be hard to control on narrow roads. Older styles, including "canned ham" trailers with a shape exactly like their namesake, are some of the most distinctive styles among vintage camper trailers. Even small versions include most of the amenities glampers prefer, including bathrooms with showers, full kitchens and dinettes, and multiple sleeping areas.

TRAVEL TRAILER

PROS
Lots of sizes and features to choose from
Easy to hitch and unhitch
Can be used while unhitched

CONS
Larger models can be difficult to tow

Travel trailers are meant to be disengaged from the tow vehicle when camping, so that they can be leveled, and the tow vehicle used for quick trips.

FIFTH WHEEL

PROS

Lots of space and amenities
Easier to tow than a travel trailer

CONS

Requires heavy-duty vehicle
Fewer retro or stylish options than other types

FIFTH WHEEL. A specialized type of towing trailer, the fifth-wheel camper is equipped with a heavy-duty tongue that is mated to a plate platform mounted in the bed of a pickup. Fifth wheels are the largest towable camper trailers and just one step shy of a full-size mobile home (with all the same amenities). Although usually larger, they are often easier to tow than travel trailers because the fifth-wheel plate is fixed over the rear axle—higher than the trailer's center of gravity—eliminating the sway common with ball-hitch trailers. However, fifth-wheel trailers require heavy-duty tow vehicles with big engines and beefy suspensions. They are also the newest technology in camper trailers, so if you're looking for retro style, you'll find fewer vintage fifth-wheel trailers than other types. Choosing a fifth wheel is a matter of committing to the tricky navigation of such a long vehicle and the horsepower necessary to pull it, in a tradeoff for the pure luxury and interior spaciousness of the trailer—which can quite easily be a long-term home on wheels. "Toy haulers" are more modern versions with rear access ramps and storage areas for larger take-alongs like dirt bikes.

You always know a fifth-wheel trailer when you see one: the nose projects over the bed of the tow vehicle.

CAMPER TRAILER ANATOMY

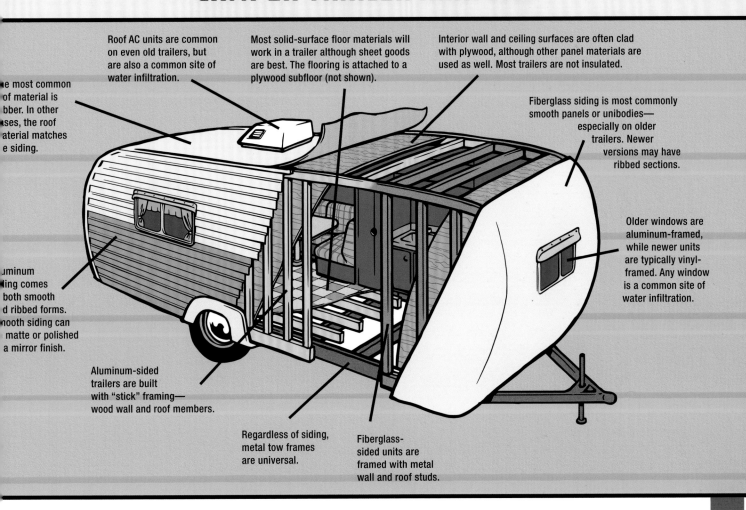

Roof AC units are common on even old trailers, but are also a common site of water infiltration.

Most solid-surface floor materials will work in a trailer although sheet goods are best. The flooring is attached to a plywood subfloor (not shown).

Interior wall and ceiling surfaces are often clad with plywood, although other panel materials are used as well. Most trailers are not insulated.

Fiberglass siding is most commonly smooth panels or unibodies—especially on older trailers. Newer versions may have ribbed sections.

he most common of material is bber. In other ases, the roof aterial matches e siding.

Older windows are aluminum-framed, while newer units are typically vinyl-framed. Any window is a common site of water infiltration.

uminum ing comes both smooth d ribbed forms. nooth siding can matte or polished a mirror finish.

Aluminum-sided trailers are built with "stick" framing—wood wall and roof members.

Regardless of siding, metal tow frames are universal.

Fiberglass-sided units are framed with metal wall and roof studs.

Once you've decided on a camper type that makes sense for your life and leisure time, you can begin your search. That's perhaps one of the most fun parts of the adventure because there is such a variety from which to choose. The trick, however, is to find a used camper trailer that is not worse for the wear. An insightful inspection and analysis of potential candidates is key, and you will find all the information you need to start your own camper hunt in the next chapter.

CLASSIC CAMPER BRANDS

From the 1940s through today, there have been dozens of camper trailer manufacturers. Some were renowned for one style of trailer, while others have manufactured multiple lines, sizes, and styles. This is far from a comprehensive list, but it is a good overview of the most enduring brands you're likely to find in the used marketplace.

AIRSTREAM

The most iconic camper trailer in history was born in 1929, when Airstream's founder built his very first trailer. It was a teardrop, with little more than an ice chest and stove and some room to spread sleeping bags. The company expanded from there, eventually developing the classic Curtis Clipper, Torpedo, and Bambi, among many other models. The "bullet-shaped," rounded, aluminum-clad trailers continue to be produced with the same timeless look and updated features, but vintage models are prized for their detailing and durability. Devotees are called "Airstreamers."

Courtesy of Airstream Inc.

ALASKAN

R. D. Hall founded the company after he built his own truck camper. Alaskans were revered for their ingenuity and craftsmanship. These were the first truck campers to feature pop-up roofs that added headroom inside. Comfort was key at Alaskan, accounting for the wide popularity of the campers.

APACHE

Gene Vesely wanted to improve on the feeble pop-up trailer designs available locally when he built his first trailer in 1957. Although they were the original camper trailers, pop-ups hadn't advanced much from their roots in the 1930s. But by building in special features and focusing on quality, Vesely's company quickly became a leading manufacturer of pop-ups. Although the earliest Apaches featured wood bases and canvas uppers, the company eventually produced some of the earliest hard-sided pop-ups and ABS plastic hard-sided camper trailers. The company went out of business in 1987.

BETHANY

This plucky Minneapolis company produced sturdy pop-up trailers from 1958 to 1985. The boxy bodies held abundant room in the pop-up, tent-like top structures, and the reliable nature of the simple campers makes this a continually popular, low-cost, vintage trailer option.

BOLER

This Canadian company started producing unique tow-behind trailers in 1968. The company molded a top and a bottom half out of fiberglass and then joined them, avoiding many of the seams that lead to leaks in trailers. Compact yet comfortable, the trailers look a little like a VW van that has had the front end cut off.

CAPRI

Manufactured since 1969, Capri has the distinction of being the first producer of cab-over campers explicitly marketed to rodeo riders. That's why the brand's most basic models are just a bunkhouse that sits in a truck bed. The modest accessories translate to affordability, and Capri campers have always been known for rugged durability. The company is still manufacturing two models—the famous basic Cowboy and the more luxurious Retreat. You'll know a Capri by the tufted diamond exterior surface.

Courtesy of Capri Camper

COACHMAN

Coachman was founded in 1964 and made their bones by building sturdy, dependable truck campers and tow-behind travel trailers. They've gone on to produce motorhomes, but they also maintain a line of travel trailers in various sizes through their new owner, Forest River.

COLEMAN

Yes, that Coleman. Famous for camping gear and their iconic campsite lamp (the company was founded in 1900 specifically to sell the lamp), Coleman began producing pop-up camper trailers in 1966. The product lines have grown through a couple of ownership changes, and the brand is still used on luxury tow-behind travel trailers.

DUTCHMEN

This relative newcomer was founded in 1988 and has produced retro-style tow-behinds that fall right between a teardrop and a canned-ham trailer. The trailer balances small luxuries and eminent practicality. They are cool, relatively lightweight, and maneuverable, and retain a flair that continues to draw many new aficionados. Although the company, now owned by industry giant Thor, has gone on to manufacture motorhomes, it's the smaller, older trailers that DIYers prize.

HALLMARK

This family-run company was founded in 1958 to produce truck campers in both traditional style and with pop-up tops that can be expanded for use and lowered for travel, to increase clearance and reduce wind drag. The company continues to produce truck campers, including models for long, short, and even imported truck beds. But the older models feature the distinctive styling of the period.

HOLIDAY RAMBLER

Although now known for its full line of motorhomes, Holiday Rambler produced travel trailers from its founding in 1953. The company made a name for itself as one of the first manufacturers to include luxury features like built-in refrigerators in its lines of fifth-wheel and tow-behind camper trailers.

JAYCO

Beginning in 1968, Jayco began producing pop-up camper trailers that were advertised as "America's Most Livable RVs." Hard as that claim may be to prove, fans certainly find even early Jaycos reliable and well outfitted. The company currently produces pop-ups and travel trailers, as well as RVs. But used Jaycos are still widely available and can represent good value for the money (depending on just how used they are).

KOMFORT

Although now owned by the corporate powerhouse Thor Industries, Komfort first started producing travel trailers on its own in 1966. They built their reputation on quality, and older Komfort travel trailers are some of the largest vintage tow-behinds you can find and were some of the most luxurious of their time.

KROWN

Although only produced from the early 1970s through 1980, the Krown pop-up trailers have stood the test of time, and many are still on the road. There isn't a lot of customization that can be done to a Krown, but the models are known for their light weight (a big plus during the bad old OPEC days) and range of sizes.

LANCE

Operating since 1966, Lance has produced high-quality truck and trailer campers for decades. The availability of vintage Lance campers—especially older truck campers—is a testament to the durability of the company's products. Lance continues to produce truck, trailer, and toy hauler campers, and remains a source of information for owners of older Lance campers.

LARK

In business for a relatively short period covering the 1960s and 1970s, Lark actually produced an astoundingly diverse line of campers and RVs. The vintage marketplace, however, is most likely to feature their boxy, spacious travel trailers. These can be considered wonderful blank slates on which to design a distinctive camper. The company went out of business in 1978, so that's the most recent model year you'll find.

NORTHSTAR

Since 1955, Northstar has made affordable truck campers, and their lines have included both pop-up and hardwall units for different sizes of truck beds. The higher end of their product line includes luxury features.

NU-WA

Although well known as a manufacturer of truck campers and motorhomes since 1969, Nu-Wa is best known to vintage camper fans for its line of Hitchhiker travel trailers. These have stood the test of time and are currently available in a number of different sizes.

PALOMINO

The earliest Palominos were "tent" pop-up trailers, but the company is perhaps most widely known for their truck campers, which have a reputation for durability and wealth of features. The company continues to produce pop-ups, truck campers, travel trailers, and fifth wheels under their current parent, Forest River.

PROWLER

Although Prowler produced fifth wheels and travel trailers through its demise in 2009, perhaps their coolest travel trailers date from the 1970s. Those classics have a boxy, angular shape that translates to loads of interior space. The aluminum siding is easily painted with retro color schemes, and the cheesy period interiors are ideal for renovation in a personal style—all of which makes Prowlers favorites for glampers.

ROCKWOOD

Beginning in 1972, Rockwood produced reliable travel trailers that, if not full of flair, were good workhorses. The company grew and was eventually acquired by industry powerhouse Forest River; the Rockwood line now includes "ultralight" trailers with all the modern conveniences one could want. Older Rockwood campers can be considered blank slates for the creative imagination.

SERRO-SCOTTY

You can just call them "Scottys," as most fans do. This much-beloved trailer was first produced by retired car salesman John Serro in 1956. The company would go on to produce the Sportsman line of trailers sold to hunters, as well as both smooth aluminum and corrugated trailers. (The Sportsman Sr. is what most collectors consider the typical Scotty, with a kitchen and full sleeping quarters.) After going out of business when the factory burned down, the line was revived in all its retro-style glory by Little Guy Trailers.

SHASTA

A classic postwar boom story, Shasta originally produced mobile military housing during World War II. After the war, the company switched to the fast-growing RV market, producing travel trailers and—eventually—fifth wheels and even motorhomes. The brand is most beloved by glampers for their stylish travel trailers from the 1950s and '60s, which define "camper cool."

Shastas are classically vintage and a frequent choice for glampers.

SIX-PAC

Six-Pac made truck campers from the 1960s through 2012, and early on developed a reputation for comfort. Older models are surprisingly spacious for a truck camper, and newer models are built for a variety of different-size beds.

SKAMPER

Although the Skamper brand was launched in 1959, glampers are most drawn to the pop-up campers and travel trailers of the late 1960s and early 1970s. Those models are all spacious and comfortable, if not the most luxurious vintage trailers available. A line of campers continues to be produced under the Skamper brand by Thor Industries.

SKYLINE

Although the company dates from 1951, they only began producing travel trailers in 1960. The most memorable is the Nomad, a standout travel trailer prized by glampers for its adaptability, quality of build, tough and lightweight aluminum frames, and diversity of sizes.

SPARTAN

The Spartan Aircraft Company started business in 1928, but went into high-gear production making aircraft for the war effort. In 1945, the company turned to producing aluminum-clad travel trailers that looked like they were moving even when they were standing still. Although Airstream is the brand most associated with polished aluminum trailers, Spartan trailers are every bit as eye-catching and distinctive. They are prized by glampers for their stylish detailing and spacious interiors.

SPORTSMEN

This is a more recent brand dating from the 1980s and is still in business. The company is known for making simple, durable units, and older Sportsmen campers can be a blank slate for glampers looking to go a bit wild in customizing a camper.

STARCRAFT

Originally producing pop-up campers with a crank to open the unit, Starcraft grew from that original product line to its current production of travel trailers and fifth wheels. But fans of retro most appreciate the full-featured late 1960s pop-ups.

TERRY

Terry is a favorite of the vintage camper enthusiast, especially Terry travel trailers dating from the 1960s. The company produced models from the very compact to larger, more luxurious units. Production stopped in 2009, but there are many older Terrys on the marketplace, and they are prime for renovation by glampers.

VACATIONEER

In business from 1965 to 1991, Vacationeer produced travel trailers and fifth wheels that have stood the test of time. They were long considered the "camper's trailer," because of their many thoughtful features. The somewhat bland, boxy design and shape lends itself to glamperizing.

WINNEBAGO

Long before Winnebago became synonymous with "mobile home," the company produced truck campers and travel trailers. In fact, starting in the 1960s, those were how the company made its name. These are the stereotypical, rough and tumble, rounded, corrugated-sided canned-ham standards of the industry that your Aunt Bev and Uncle Bill probably used in pure happiness for decades.

The Winnebago Dot trailer.

UNDERSTANDING, ASSESSING, and CHOOSING A USED CAMPER

A pop-up is a good choice for frequent weekenders who want to bring some amenities with them, usually camp at established campsites, and are otherwise comfortable spending most of the time out of the camper.

The perfect camping adventure starts with buying the perfect camper trailer—specifically, the perfect one for you. That's a tall order, because manufacturers, especially manufacturers of older campers, don't know you. They probably would have liked to meet you, but your particular needs and preferences unfortunately didn't figure into what they built. That means you'll have to work backward, finding exactly the trailer with the space and amenities that accommodate the way you want to camp.

Any camper search is also limited somewhat by the vehicle you hope to use to transport your new (to you) camper. Pickup owners are lucky; they can choose from any style except fifth wheel (unless they're willing to foot the hefty expense of retrofitting their truck bed with a fifth-wheel receiver and the suspension can take the added weight). Want to use your cherry '42 coupe to pull the camper? You'll have to restrict your search to tow-behinds, like pop-ups, travel trailers, and teardrops that don't weigh more than the car can reasonably pull.

Length of stay and travel distance will be two other key factors in your choice of camper. Although any given camper type can be used for many different types of camping trip, the table at right is a general guide to the type of stay for which each style was intended.

WHAT'S YOUR IDEAL INTERIOR SPACE?

Deciding on how much space you need inside a camper isn't quite as easy as determining a home's usability by looking at the square footage—space inside a camper is a flexible notion. To start with, some campers have slide-out partitions that can increase the area inside drastically, sometimes doubling it. Second, if you intend on spending most of your vacation time on day hikes or away from the camper, the interior space is less important than it would be if you hope to make the camper an indoor room at a campsite or actually your primary residence for an extended period of time. Make sure you're taking these things into consideration when you weigh the pros and cons of different camper sizes.

Length and Type of Stay	Best Camper
Occasional overnight stay with friends	Teardrop or pop-up
Long weekends at a full-service campground	Truck camper
Weeklong trips to wild and scenic areas with limited services	14' to 20' travel trailer
Cross-country trips and multiweek vacations to rugged outdoor areas	28' to 44' travel trailer or fifth wheel

The straight, linear layout with bunks at each end of the camper is one of the most common floor plans—but far from the only style. Depending on how extensive your rehab gumption is, you may entirely redesign the interior space.

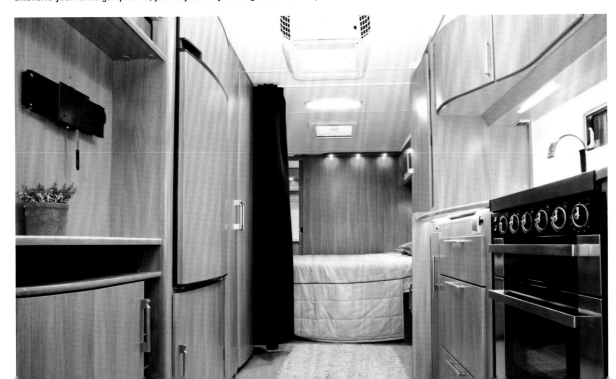

SAMPLE FLOOR PLANS

The floor plans shown here represent common sizes and configurations for the different types of camper trailers. Keep in mind that these are baselines, meant to give you a rough idea of the dimensions of each camper type (none here, for instance, shows slide-outs, which are fairly common on larger, newer trailers). There are an amazing amount of variations in the marketplace among each type of camper. You can often find manuals with floor plans for vintage campers with an online search, but if you can't find anything for a camper you're considering, make a quick sketch when you tour it. Most importantly, measure the length of the bed; RV mattresses are often custom sizes that may not work for tall people.

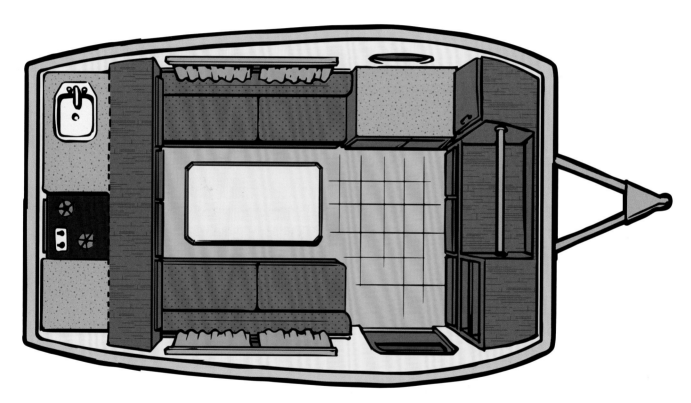

TEARDROP   Sleeps: 4   Length: 11'11" (including hitch structure)   Width: 6'6"   Weight (empty): 800 lb.

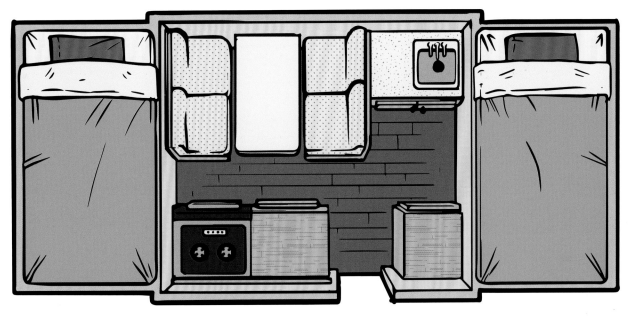

POP-UP   Sleeps: 4   Length: 15' (including hitch structure)   Width: 6'8"   Weight (empty): 700 lb.

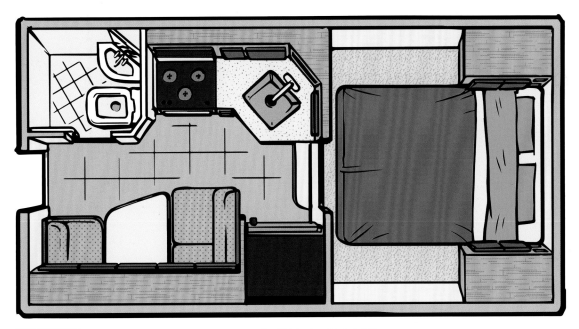

TRUCK CAMPER   Sleeps: 3–4   Length: 16'6"   Width: 8'1"   Weight (empty): 2,150 lb.

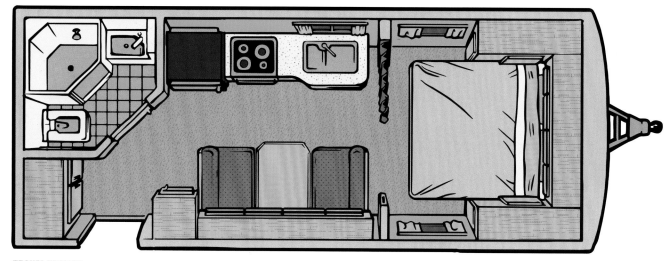

TRAVEL TRAILER   Sleeps: 4–6   Length: 14'8" (including hitch structure)   Width: 6'6"   Weight (empty): 1,480 lb.

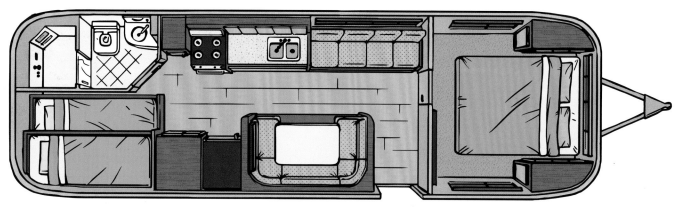

FIFTH-WHEEL CAMPER TRAILER   Sleeps: 6   Length: 28' (including hitch structure)   Width: 8'6"   Weight (empty): 8,235 lb.

After you settle the broader issues of the size and type of camper that suit you best, it's time to give some thought to the specific camper features you want. That decision-making process starts from the outside.

PICK YOUR SKIN

Camper siding is not necessarily something you'll have much say in; your choices may be limited by the used campers available in your local marketplace. Additionally, if you're interested in one particular brand—like Airstream—the decision has already been made for you. But where there is more than one candidate on your wish list, siding may sway you toward one or the other. Whichever type you wind up with, always remember that the condition of and coating on a camper's "skin" determine whether your home on wheels is eye candy or an eyesore. Siding also plays a super important role as the first line of defense against any camper's arch nemesis: water.

Although pop-ups are mostly fabric sided, if the camper of your dreams is any other style, it will usually have one of the two basic solid-siding types: aluminum or synthetic.

ALUMINUM

Early camper trailers were commonly clad in shiny, sexy aircraft aluminum left over from factories shifting out of fighter-plane production and into more practical consumer goods in the postwar period of the late 1940s. Polished aluminum panels are still used on high-end trailers, but more often than not, aluminum siding comes in the form of shaped (corrugated or bent) and painted panels. These have been common across low- and mid-priced trailers throughout history. Flat aluminum panels were

Smooth, polished aluminum panels make for some of the most beautiful trailer exteriors. However, this type of skin requires a lot of maintenance.

Beautiful two-tone paint jobs are one of the advantages of shaped aluminum panels, like the ones on this new, retro-style canned ham trailer.
Courtesy CH Camper Company

riveted to the frame and to each other. Shaped panels were screwed in place and are much easier to replace. In either case, aluminum is applied over a wood frame similar to a home's skeleton. It's why these are sometimes called "stick-and-tin" trailers.

Aluminum won't deform in temperature extremes and will expand and contract modestly under variations in temperature. Properly maintained, the metal has a long life, and polished aluminum is an undeniably cool look. However, the wood framing is susceptible to rot and mold from even minor leaks (although the construction makes it easier to take apart a section and replace sticks). On the plus side, stick-and-tin construction makes it easier to add blocking for a retrofit installation such as a window. If the exterior surface is dented or punctured—a common form of damage—shaped panels are removed and replaced at moderate cost, while smooth panels will need to be deconstructed, making repair prohibitively expensive. In general, aluminum campers cost less than those with fiberglass or synthetic siding (but are heavier, and add to fuel costs as a tradeoff).

SYNTHETIC

There are two types of synthetic camper trailer skins: fiberglass and composite. Both are used on trailers at every price point, but older campers and most new ones will be fiberglass. Lightweight, inexpensive, and durable, synthetic siding comes both smooth and corrugated. Yesterday's fiberglass shells were prone to UV damage, including fading, delamination (the layers of the siding separating from one another), and other problems. More contemporary formulations build in a lot of UV protection. Fiberglass and composite trailer shells can be painted, but they are also formed with an inherent color that is sometimes decorated with adhesive

The vast majority of camper trailers produced today are made of fiberglass. The smooth sides are easy to clean, and new formulations hold up well under exposure to the elements. Older fiberglass trailers commonly have shaped siding similar to corrugated aluminum trailer siding.

tape or appliqués. However, a painted synthetic skin will resist sun damage better than an unpainted version. Fiberglass skin also stays cleaner because the surface is smoother than shaped aluminum and doesn't attract the oxidation polished aluminum will.

Synthetic skins are used in what is known as laminate trailer construction. The fiberglass or composite is molded into sheet form and then laminated to a bonding surface—usually a wood substrate—to form custom-size panels or actual shells, although certain types of campers are manufactured from molded sections to create a monocoque body. The panels or shells are typically attached to a metal frame, which hikes up the total cost of the trailer, lowers the overall weight, and lessens the chance of rot from water infiltration.

Direct price comparisons are difficult to make. You'll pay more for a fiberglass camper trailer, but it will probably cost you less in gas over the long run. The one major drawback to both fiberglass and composites is laminate integrity. Weeklong vacations in the heart of Death Valley, or a winter romp through the freezing temperatures in the High Sierras, can stress synthetic surfaces, causing them to blister, crack, deform, or separate from the underlying bonding surface. That's especially a problem with older trailers (newer formulas and methods of lamination handle temperature variations much better). However, this is not a substantial problem with older molded fiberglass trailers.

OVERHEAD COSTS

One of the great things about a camper is having a roof over your head when you're far from civilization. Sure, you might not see the stars for the four minutes before you fall into a deep, outdoor-air-fueled slumber, but all other things being equal, it sure beats being rained on.

The thing is, a camper's roof takes a lot of abuse. It's subject to the same stresses and strains that the rest of the structure is, but also has to hold up to prolonged UV exposure, torrential downpours, hail, snow pack, and more. Because most campers won't fit in the average garage, your trailer usually has to endure these insults year-round. No wonder the roof is the most common point of origin for water infiltration. That makes your initial inspection of a camper's roof incredibly important, and it's why you need to understand what you're looking at. Understanding the material and construction of a trailer's roof is the only way that you can properly assess the roof's true condition.

If you're considering a truly vintage camper, there's a good possibility that the roof is made of the same stuff as the siding. However, if you're in the market for something a little newer, you'll probably be looking at a rubber top surface. Rubber roofs became the most common camper roofing material about twenty-five years ago. For any camper made from that point forward, if it wasn't rubber, it was probably fiberglass. Although any type of rubber is lower cost and lighter weight than either a fiberglass or an aluminum roof, rubber does require a lot more maintenance.

Fiberglass roofs are, surprisingly, prone to oxidation. But whether the roof is fiberglass, aluminum, or rubber, regular cleanings with products meant specifically for the particular surface are key to roof longevity and heading off any potential problems.

The roof of a camper takes a lot of abuse. It can be easy for it to fall prey to "out of sight, out of mind," but a poorly maintained roof can mean cracks and leaks—which can mean water damage and other problems.

Camper rubber roofs typically last between fifteen and twenty years, depending on how well they are maintained. It's hard to determine the actual age unless you're sure it's the original roof, or the owner kept records of the roof's replacement. The first order of business is to determine what type of rubber roof it is. The options are ethylene propylene diene monomer (EPDM) a nd thermoplastic olefin (TPO). EPDM is much more common. Unlike TPO, EPDM is specifically formulated to oxidize over time and exposure to the elements, as a protective feature. An EPDM will "shed" white or gray residue in streaks along the sides of the camper, which should be regularly washed off. Another telltale sign is that EPDM becomes slick when wet; TPO roofing does not.

Whatever the material, it's important to get up on the roof to inspect it. Just remember that it's always better to be safe than sorry. Wear light shoes, such as sneakers, and make darn sure the soles are clean before getting up on the roof. Unless you're fond of slides and serious injury, only inspect the roof when it's dry.

Look closely at all the seals or caulking around the rooftop fixtures, including air-conditioning units, vents, skylights and roof windows, antennas or satellite dishes, and the top mounts for ladders. The caulk or sealant around openings should be intact— no cracking, checking, or missing sections. Also eyeball the seams. There should be no signs of separation, splitting, rust, rot, or water stains. If the overall surface appears oxidized and sunworn, don't be overly concerned; there are many cleaners and polishers meant specifically for each type of roofing, and oxidation is a pretty normal side effect of regular weather exposure.

TOW FRAME AND SUSPENSION

Unless you're shopping exclusively for a truck camper, you'll have to pay careful attention to the tow frame on which the camper's body is mounted. That base, a metal grid that is fronted with a V terminating in the hitch, is essential to the safety and longevity of the rest of the structure. Pay close attention to the condition of the frame itself; the overall wear and tear on the tires, rims, and brakes; and the integrity of the frame and hitch structures.

TOW FRAME

Whether it's a modest pop-up or a jumbo 30-foot travel trailer, the tow frame mediates some intense forces—from twisty torsion to flexing shear loads to heavy quick-stop compression. If the previous owner fancied him- or herself an off-roader, venturing into rugged, untamed terrain with the trailer, the tow frame probably took the brunt of the punishment. (See the inspection guide on page 56 for the specific damage you need to be on the lookout for.)

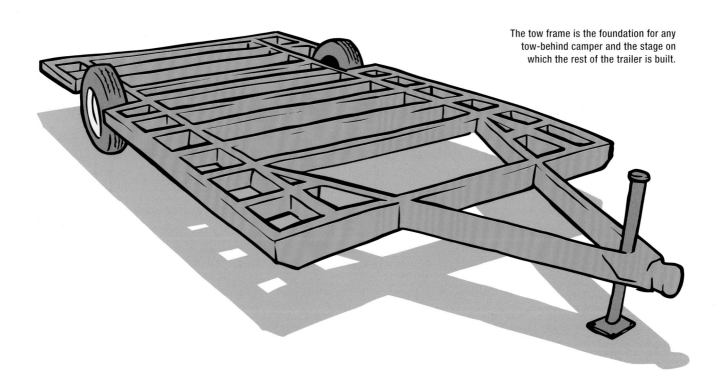

The tow frame is the foundation for any tow-behind camper and the stage on which the rest of the trailer is built.

JACKS AND LEVELERS

When parked, trailers need to be leveled and stabilized to make them as comfortable as possible and keep the systems working as they should. Smaller trailers such as pop-ups and teardrops, especially older ones, may have simple unattached scissor jacks that are placed at the front, or front and rear, under the frame. The bodies of these campers are often equipped with simple bubble levels. Travel trailers usually have a telescoping jack at the tip of the tow frame behind the actual hitch connection. These are most often hand-operated and used in conjunction with a built-in level or a separate level inside the camper. Fifth wheels and the front of truck campers are equipped with telescoping jacks for the same purpose. But in the case of most fifth wheels, those jacks will be hydraulically powered using the trailer's battery. Some even have an automatic leveler. Checking the jacks that are used with the trailer is key to a trailer inspection.

TIRES AND BRAKES

They may not look like much, but those camper trailer tires are pretty dang important. Just like you can put lipstick on a pig, tires can be dressed up to disguise cracking and other signs of age. So they'll be an important part of any prepurchase inspection. Keep in mind that sidewall failure is a bigger danger than tread wear on camper trailer tires (although the type of tread wear can tell you some interesting stories about the other parts of the suspension; see page 80 for insight on reading tire tread).

First and foremost, though, the tires should be the proper type. Tires made specifically for camper trailers will carry the designation "ST" (special tire) on the sidewall. An "LT" means a light truck tire is being used. They are not comparable, because an ST tire is designed for the particular stresses of a towed camper, which other tires are not. The tires on both sides should be exactly the same type, size, construction, make, and model. Age is the most important factor in considering the tires, and unless the current owner of the camper has detailed records, you may not be able to discern the age of the tires.

Time is more an indicator of tire life or death than mileage. Most authorities believe that camper tires should last somewhere between three and eight years, although the majority of professionals recommend replacing any camper tire that is five years or older. Like you and me, tires should not spend their time sitting around. Camper tires last longer when they are regularly in use. If a camper becomes a driveway fixture, the rubber can dry out and degrade under the exposure

Don't forget to inspect the tires on a prospective camper purchase.

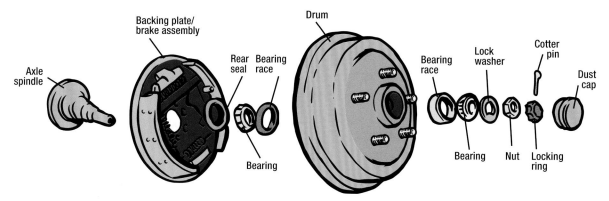

This exploded diagram shows a common camper drum brake assembly—the relationship between the hub, brakes, and bearings. However, there are many variations, and yours may differ somewhat from the diagram.

to UV light and temperature variations. Another thing that many camper owners and potential camper owners fail to understand is that the tires, just like a car or truck tire, should be balanced. Unbalanced camper tires not only have shorter lives, but they can also cause a variety of problems in the camper itself from excessive vibration. If the sidewalls show significant cracking, add new tires to the purchase price.

Brakes are essential as well, because if the trailer keeps moving when the car tries to stop, all kinds of bad things can happen. Most brakes on trailers, especially used trailers, are drum brakes.

The overall brake system is going to be one of two types: electric and surge. Electric brakes operate at the same moment the tow vehicle's brakes are applied, by an electric signal that is routed through an electric brake controller when the tow vehicle's brake pedal is depressed. Surge brakes are an older and less efficient system; they work by compression. As the tow vehicle slows after braking, a piston compresses and triggers the trailer's brakes.

HITCHES

Your hitch determines—in part—the camper weight that your tow vehicle can pull. Obviously, that weight limit is also contingent on the actual rating for any given vehicle (you can check with your car or truck's manual, or look online for internet databases). But even if you own a heavy-duty truck capable of hauling ginormous loads, that won't mean a thing if you use an undersized trailer hitch. The hitch can easily become the weak link in the connection chain between vehicles.

Trailer hitches are universal, so the variable is the hitch receiver that's attached to your car or truck. If you're buying a used camper, you'll have to decide whether to stick with the hitch you have or upgrade. Fixed-drawbar hitches are less popular than others because they stick out awkwardly from the rear bumper, causing problems when a trailer is not attached. The "receiver" style is more common and is sometimes called a "box" or "tube" hitch. You'll need the latter if you're using any kind of weight-distributing system—a wonderful safety feature when towing medium-size or large trailers.

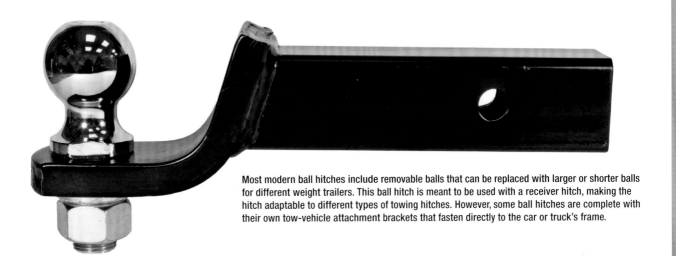

Most modern ball hitches include removable balls that can be replaced with larger or shorter balls for different weight trailers. This ball hitch is meant to be used with a receiver hitch, making the hitch adaptable to different types of towing hitches. However, some ball hitches are complete with their own tow-vehicle attachment brackets that fasten directly to the car or truck's frame.

A receiver can accept a square tongue or can be fitted with a slip-in ball attachment. In either case, the male end is secured in the hitch with an oversized cotter pin or large bolt. *CURT Manufacturing*

A gooseneck offers the handling advantages of a fifth wheel for trailers, with a small extension on the front end (usually housing a cramped loft bed). This particular version can be adjusted on its mounting rails or completely removed as necessary. *CURT Manufacturing*

The most secure type of hitch with the best handling and anti-sway characteristics, the fifth wheel also requires a bed for mounting. Detachable fifth wheels are available that allow the owner to use the truck bed for other purposes. *CURT Manufacturing*

THE FIFTH-WHEEL ALTERNATIVE

The gooseneck hitch is an alternative to a fifth wheel, and is meant to combine the best of a fifth wheel and a ball hitch. The hitch is a ball that sticks up in the bed of the pickup, directly over the rear axle. The ball is attached to a frame underneath the bed, which is in turn attached to the truck's frame. An extension post connects the fifth wheel yoke on a trailer to the ball in the bed of the truck. The gooseneck is not as sturdy a connection as a true fifth wheel, which is why most states dictate that no one can be in the trailer when towing with a gooseneck, while they can be if towing with a fifth wheel. But a gooseneck does eliminate the sway associated with a conventional ball hitch and is less expensive than a fifth-wheel setup. A big advantage is that the ball can be detached, leaving the truck's bed entirely usable whenever it's not towing the trailer.

Fifth wheels are the other type of tow attachment, and are meant specifically for towing heavier loads beyond class 3 or 4 (the designations given to tow hitches based on the weight they're capable of pulling). A receiver plate is mounted to the bed of a pickup truck, and a yoke attached to the trailer is slid into the mating slot in the plate. The yoke is locked in place, and a safety cable is used as a fail-safe, connecting the truck to the camper. Fifth-wheel mechanisms are, like tow hitches, universal, and rated by weight limit. The benefit to any fifth wheel is that it eliminates trailer sway, making it much easier and safer to pull a trailer of any length—but especially longer trailers.

If you're a fifth-wheel kind of outdoorsperson, you need to make sure the hitch yoke on the trailer is undamaged. You should also connect the trailer to your fifth wheel before buying, to ensure that the connection is established easily. Hook up the electrical connection from the tow vehicle to make sure the trailer brakes and lights work as they should (something you should also test with a ball hitch connection).

SYSTEMS

Most people expect their camper trailers to be something more than a shell that they can lie down in at the end of a long, fun day in the outdoors. Functions, from bathing to cooking, are part of the appeal of any camper. Those functions rely on basic systems that are, to one degree or another, similar to the systems that serve a home. Camper systems are fairly simple, but they need to be in good repair for any camper trailer to be worth the asking price.

PROPANE

The most common source of power for camper appliances is liquid propane (LP), which is stored in pressurized steel tanks. The most common setup for travel trailers is a two-tank system, with the tanks mounted on the tongue of the tow hitch frame, but some smaller models have just a single tank. Truck campers and fifth wheels usually have a special enclosed and ventilated compartment for the tanks. Any camper LP system will be basic in design, but there are several points that can fail or cause problems in the system as a whole. Regular testing and maintenance are essential to ensure not only uninterrupted operation but also, more importantly, camper safety.

Propane tanks can range in capacity from less than 10 pounds to more than 40, but the basic design of the system doesn't change. Gas flows out of a tank, through a regulator that controls line pressure, out to solenoids that control flow and can shut off the gas supply, and through supply hoses to appliances that can include a water heater, furnace, space heaters, refrigerator, and stove.

The tanks are the first, most important part of the system. Camper trailers must use tanks certified by the Department of Transportation (DOT), and the

Although older camper trailers often include exposed propane tanks, it's wise to use a cover similar to the one shown here. Propane tanks are subject to deterioration over time and exposure to the elements, and they're not inexpensive to replace.

tanks are given an expiration date past which they cannot be refilled. The hoses, regulator, pressure gauge, and fittings can all be potential trouble spots: a broken or malfunctioning regulator can lead to a dangerous pressure buildup in the system, fixtures and hoses can leak, and the pressure gauge can register incorrect readings.

A physical check of the tanks is the first order of business. Look for any noticeable scratches, cracks, deterioration of seams, or pervasive rust. Check the date stamped on the tank's collar. Propane tanks must be either recycled or recertified after twelve years. A tank older than that cannot be refilled unless there is a new certification sticker on the tank. (Certification costs far less than new tanks.) So, in other words, if the tanks look beat up and are close to the twelve-year mark, you may be staring at an additional couple of hundred dollars in the short term.

The regulator should also be checked before a camper purchase. A certified technician does this anywhere in the system, by attaching a measuring device called a "manometer." The manometer measures the pressure in the form of water column inches, and the technician adjusts, repairs, or replaces the regulator accordingly.

There are other tests certified technicians perform to ensure there are no leaks in an LP system. That's why you should have the system checked out by a technician whenever you're looking to purchase a used camper trailer. Keep in mind that LP system maintenance and malfunctions are *not* DIY issues. If you encounter a problem, put your pride aside, keep your toolbox in the garage, and make an appointment with a certified technician.

HOT WATER

Water heaters are luxury items in any camper. Toasty showers and a supply of hot water to wash dishes are among the key must-haves that separate happy campers from their "roughing-it" brethren. Camper hot water heaters are really the twins to gas-powered home units. Although the units can, in fact, be powered by electricity or propane, most are propane fired because of the plentiful supply available in most campers. As in a home, the actual size of the heater limits the amount of hot water available at any given time. They range from 4-gallon to 20-gallon capacity, and you should assess how well the heater in the camper you're considering will meet the needs and showering preferences of your own camping posse. If certain individuals—who will remain nameless—fancy a long, luxurious shower after that 5-mile hike, you'll be looking at a 15- to 20-gallon water heater (or upgrading that unit that is currently in the camper). As with home water heaters, any camper water heater should come equipped with an anode rod that prevents corrosion of the heater walls. If it doesn't have one, plan on replacing the drain plug with an anode rod.

PLUMBING AND SEWAGE

Seems like a no-brainer, right? Why wouldn't you want a commode in your campsite on wheels? Buy a camper without one and you'll save a good deal of money but be at the mercy of campground facilities that may be, well, less than luxurious. That's why these are the most make-or-break features for many used-camper shoppers.

Any camper with a faucet will have a freshwater tank, and that same tank will serve the bathroom, supplying water for showering (after it passes through a water heater) and flushing the toilet. But a camper with a functional bathroom will be equipped with two other tanks—a gray water and a black water tank. Gray water is where water from dishwashers, sinks, and showers is drained. The black water tank? That's the unmentionable container that serves as your onboard sewer; only the toilet drains into that one. The size of all the tanks correlates to the size of the trailer. If you opt for a camper with a toilet, you'll be dealing with the gray and black water tanks sooner rather than later.

The gray and black water tanks must be regularly emptied into a sewer by way of dump or sanitation stations, which are available at many RV parks. Always empty your tanks before traveling to lighten the weight of the trailer. The black water tank is emptied first, by connecting a hose to the dump station at one end and the tank's valve at the other, using a special odor-capturing fitting. The valve is then opened to drain the tank. The process is repeated on the gray water tank, which ensures the hose is flushed of solid matter. Both tanks are also periodically cleaned and flushed, and winterized over colder months when the camper will be unused for extended periods.

High-quality waste hoses and fittings are essential for trouble-free emptying of waste tanks.

When inspecting a camper you might want to buy, be sure to sit on the toilet. RV toilets are generally shorter than home thrones, and if the toilet is extremely uncomfortable, it may actually play into your decision to buy or not buy. Flush the toilet to ensure the flush is strong and reliable. Check the tank outlet valve on the outside of the camper; it should be relatively clean and odor free or the current owner has not been following accepted sanitary practices—not a good sign.

Wet rooms are combinations of shower and toilet. In smaller campers, such as some pop-ups, this may be as simple as a shroud curtain that is pulled up to the ceiling, allowing you to shower while sitting on the toilet. In other cases, it's a small room where you have to stand over the toilet to shower. In either case, carefully judge whether you'll be okay with accommodating the cramped shower quarters on long camping trips.

Travel trailers and fifth wheels usually have a separate shower enclosure. When evaluating one of these, take your shoes off and stand in the enclosure. Taller people often don't comfortably fit in camper shower stalls. This may or may not be a big deal for you, depending on the type of camping you plan on doing, how dirty you'll get in your outdoor adventures, and how much you have to contort to take a shower. In any case, test the ventilation fans for both the shower and the bathroom to ensure they still strongly draw air. Weak fans will need to be replaced.

Be aware that, if you're considering a camper with a "wet room" (combined toilet and shower), everything in the room will get wet when you shower. The room should be equipped with a shroud over the toilet paper, and minimal storage for obvious reasons. At first glance, you might be a little put off by the cramped confines of a wet room, but don't rush to judgment. Many campers end up liking their wet rooms, because they can sit while showering, and the room is cleaned each time they are. If you go that direction, it's a good idea to keep a squeegee on a plastic hook over the toilet; use it to remove moisture from all the surfaces after each shower.

THE CASSETTE OPTION

Some pop-ups, truck campers, and other smaller travel trailers simply don't have the space for a black water tank. But they can still have a bathroom, using what's known as a "cassette" toilet. (This is also a fairly easy and affordable retrofit for older trailers that don't currently have a bathroom at all.) A cassette toilet is basically a bench seat with a funnel that terminates in what looks like a rolling piece of luggage—the cassette. This is commonly a 4- to 5-gallon holding tank that, when full, is disengaged and removed. Unlike a true black water tank that has to be hooked up to an approved dump station, the cassette can be emptied

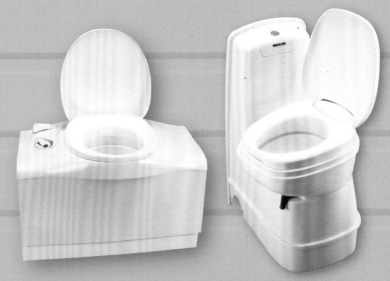

Cassette toilets are used in smaller campers that can't accommodate full-size gray and black water tanks. The standard version (left) includes a molded unibody. The version at (right) features a streamlined, space-conserving shape, with a rotatable seat for maximum convenience.

anywhere solid waste drains, from a campsite sewer to a rest stop bathroom. A simple sensor lets you know when the cassette needs to be emptied. The flush water is supplied from the onboard water supply.

The downside to cassette toilets is their limited capacity: be ready to empty them a lot more frequently than you would a black water tank. This makes it a less-than-desirable option for a busy camper used by a large family. Also, there's the "eww" factor: the seal around the inlet is sometimes not perfect, which means there may be some small cleanup in the cassette closet (usually performed with antiseptic wipes and a clothespin for your nose).

ELECTRICAL SYSTEM

All but the simplest campers use a combination of electrical sources. A 12-volt battery powers the camper's 12-volt direct current (DC) system, while a parallel wiring system in the camper runs off of 120 volts of alternating current (AC)—the same as your house. Many campers, if not most, include a converter that can change direct current from a 12-volt power supply to 120-volt alternating current.

Although a camper can be powered by the tow-vehicle's 12-volt system by way of a hookup cable, most campers have their own 12-volt battery or battery array. Check out the age and type of the existing 12-volt battery. If you plan on camping at campgrounds or locations with a 120-volt hookup for your shoreline, a standard deep-cycle battery will easily meet your needs. However, if you plan on going rogue in the great untamed outdoors, far from any plug-in (called

When checking out a camper, be sure to see what kind of power inlets is has and what kind of shape they're in.

"boondocking"), you'll probably need to upgrade to a battery with a large reserve capacity, or even a double-battery system. The charged 12-volt battery also usually provides the ignition for propane-powered appliances.

To inspect fuses and breakers for the 12-volt system, you can find them in the same compartment as the battery. Other fuses for the specific interior areas and fixtures can normally be found in the 12-volt distribution panel inside the camper. The onboard 120-volt system is run off an outside power source via the shoreline electrical cable or, in the case of larger camper trailers, by the onboard generator; the 120-volt system is usually used to power the air conditioners, microwave, and outlets throughout the camper.

When checking out a camper, see whether it features 30-amp or 50-amp service. Thirty-amp service is the most common for 120-volt systems, but it's a bit limiting because it means you can only run one appliance at a time or you risk tripping the breakers—no showering and making coffee at the same time! A 50-amp service allows you to use multiple appliances at once.

Any electrical inspection should also include the camper's outlets. Ground fault circuit interrupters (GFCIs) are standard on modern trailers because they protect against short-circuiting and fire. If the camper you're looking at doesn't have them, plan on retrofitting the interior with GFCI outlets.

HEATING

Even if you have no intention of ever camping in the winter, sooner or later you'll probably find yourself in a place with cold nights. When your teeth are chattering and there aren't enough blankets to keep you warm in your bunk is not the time to start thinking about your camper's furnace.

Like your home, some campers are heated by a furnace that can be either electric or propane powered. Propane furnaces are the most common and are highly reliable (they use electrical power to ignite, and to run circulation fans and blowers). Propane furnace systems heat the entire camper interior rather than one specific zone. This is only an issue in larger camper trailers where it would be more efficient just to warm a single area—such as the bedroom. In general, though, propane systems are not especially efficient.

Any camper that was made before the mid-1970s will most likely be a basic pilot model. These feature a pilot port fueled by the gas source and are lit manually. Direct spark ignition furnaces have largely replaced these. This type is fired by electronic ignition that provides better efficiency and more complete safety features.

Don't be bummed if the camper you have your heart set on doesn't contain a furnace. Electric heaters can be a wonderful alternative and can even be used instead of a furnace where the situation calls for heating a small area or just one person. These units are becoming increasingly popular with camping-inclined people of all stripes, but especially glampers dealing with older "canned ham" or pop-up trailers. Electric heaters allow for precise control over which area is heated when, and how warm. Plus, depending on where you park for the night, the power for an electric heater may be free, with the cost of the shoreline hookup rolled into the space rental. You can choose from among portable electric space heaters, infrared radiant heaters, and others. See page 124 for a complete, in-depth breakdown.

THE FEATURED PRESENTATION

Checking out the interior of any candidate—and imagining all the cool changes you could make to customize it to your own style and needs—is often the most enjoyable part of a camper purchase. The interior is where true glampers and fans of retro style express themselves. It's also where camper owners generally do most of their relaxing, eating, and sleeping. It pays to be on the lookout for features that make sense for you and the kind of vacationing you do.

STORAGE

It's the rare camper trailer that isn't starved for good storage. Storage might be less of an issue if you're simply looking for a mobile sleeping structure to house two people on the occasional overnight trip. But if you're an avid camper and adventurer, or have a large crew that will come along on your outdoor travels, the right amount and type of storage will be key to how much you enjoy the trailer and how easy life in the wild will be for your troop.

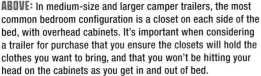

ABOVE: In medium-size and larger camper trailers, the most common bedroom configuration is a closet on each side of the bed, with overhead cabinets. It's important when considering a trailer for purchase that you ensure the closets will hold the clothes you want to bring, and that you won't be hitting your head on the cabinets as you get in and out of bed.

RIGHT: You can never have too many cabinets in a camper kitchen. Even in this confined space, cabinets make for safe and secure storage.

Closets are essential for foul-weather gear and any nicer clothes that need to be hung up. It should be noted that manufacturers were and still are very liberal with what they call a closet, and you should actually try hanging something in the so-called closet of any camper you're thinking of buying to see whether the space is actually tall and deep enough to accommodate it. Check that it is actually long enough for your size shirts and jackets, and perhaps a dress—you never know when you might be using your camper as overflow lodging at a distant wedding!

Cabinets are harder to judge until you actually use the camper, because it's difficult to tell exactly what you'll store where. Just the same, consider cabinet depth (shallow cabinets offer far less flexibility in what you can store in them) and accessibility (a cabinet that's a decent size but a pain to reach will not be much of a storage asset). Ultimately, though, keep in mind that cabinetry and shelving are awfully easy retrofits if it turns out that the storage in your dream travel trailer is simply inadequate.

Other storage features, such as racks next to sinks that keep essentials secured during travel, are an added bonus in any camper.

REFRIGERATOR

Camper refrigerators are a little different from your basic home kitchen centerpiece. For starters, the units in a camper are usually half-height, with a lot less capacity than a home model—you might have flashbacks to your college dorm. Camper refrigerators also chill food in a different way, using a process called *absorption*, in which ammonia is heated and then circulated in conjunction with other compounds to absorb heat from inside the refrigerator. This eliminates the need for a compressor and other moving parts that would quickly malfunction or deteriorate under the constant vibration of a well-traveled camper. But it also means these are fairly complex appliances. Replacement and servicing are usually left to professionals, and camper refrigerators can be pricey to replace.

Older units may be dedicated to one energy source or another, while the most common camper refrigerators are "two-way," and can switch themselves (or be switched) between electricity and propane. Modern versions can even automatically choose between 120-volt alternating current, 12-volt direct current, or propane, depending on which is available and most efficient.

RV refrigerators (the term used for all appliances meant for traveling lodgings) come in a range of sizes, measured in cubic feet. The baseline for most campers is a simple bachelor refrigerator, often without a separate freezer. (Some owners of vintage campers buy a separate icemaker.) Willing to spend some serious coin? If you have the room for it, you can upgrade to a much larger, sleeker model with a separate freezer and automatic icemaker. Upgrading to a larger and more efficient unit can run from several hundred to more than a thousand dollars. You'll also need to factor in cost of installation unless you're experienced enough to do it yourself, and you may be bumping up your energy costs. Just removing the old and installing the new can run more than a hundred dollars. That's why a refrigerator that is obviously on its last legs can be a deal breaker for used camper hunters.

Check the existing refrigerator for obvious damage. Inspect interior surfaces for cracks, holes, or seam separations. Look carefully at the seals and how tightly the door closes. Misalignment of the door, or missing, cracked, or otherwise damaged seals indicate improper care and treatment (which may be reflected in the state of the trailer at large). They can also mean the refrigerator won't properly chill food.

Measure the interior of a camper's refrigerator to get a more precise sense of the true capacity. (Capacity may differ even between two refrigerators with the same outside dimensions.) Although these units are inevitably cramped for

RV refrigerators are designed for maximum space efficiency. Even smaller units can store just about anything you could want on a camping trip. Most run on standard AC power, but some operate with propane or DC.

space, the most important consideration is whether any particular refrigerator will accommodate the must-haves you want to take on every camping trip. For instance, if a gallon-size jug of milk is a campsite essential for your Cheerios-munching family of four, you should actually check that the jug fits into the refrigerator. You'll also need to decide whether you must have a freezer compartment. Ice is a huge luxury on a camping trip and although most smaller camper refrigerators don't include an icemaker, a freezer section will allow you to keep a modest supply on hand.

Regardless of anything else, you need to make sure the refrigerator actually runs. Ask the owner to cool off the unit before you arrive to check out the camper (the process can take four to six hours). That's the only way to be absolutely certain the unit works.

Keep in mind that less-convenient portable refrigerators are available, and they can be tucked under a dinette or in another out-of-the-way location as space permits.

If luxury is your bottom line, a full-size, double-door refrigerator is a must-have in a large fifth-wheel trailer like this one.

COOKTOPS AND RANGES

Planning on cooking in your camper? Look for one equipped with a cooktop, but don't necessarily discount an otherwise attractive candidate just because the cooktop is undersized or there is no oven. You can actually accomplish of lot of simple cooking on two or three burners, and if you're going with basic cookout fare like hot dogs and burgers, you probably aren't going to make much use of an oven. However, unlike refrigerators, cooktops are relatively inexpensive and easy to upgrade or even retrofit. External, standalone camping cooktops are also widely available for very reasonable prices.

Camper ranges and cooktops are designated by fuel source. Propane stoves are the most common, but they are more dangerous than electric cooktops because the burners use an open flame and the propane itself is

A three-burner gas cooktop is common in older travel trailers, and is easy to maintain or upgrade.

highly flammable. Electric versions are somewhat less common and require an electrical hookup—if one doesn't exist you'll have to wire it in. Any camper cooktop is a simple mechanism that can be checked simply by turning it on. Each burner of a gas cooktop should produce a blue flame that is fully adjustable. Check the fittings for cracks or deformities. The burners of an electric cooktop should quickly heat up if the cooktop is properly connected to the power source.

BEDS

Comfortable sleeping quarters are one of the key benefits to a tow-behind or truck camper. After all, if you were okay with sleeping on the bare ground, why would you need a camper in the first place? The problem is, space is confined in any camper, so the industry developed mattress sizes that differ from standard home mattress dimensions. Although larger travel trailers and fifth wheels may include standard beds and mattresses, campers often incorporate smaller versions made specifically for the RV industry. These sizes are (length × width):

Queen Short = 60 × 75 inches

Three-Quarter = 48 × 75 inches

Twin = 38 × 75 inches

RV King = 72 × 80 inches

Depending on the camper's age and manufacturer, the mattress may even be a custom size. But no matter what the outside dimensions are, the ugly truth is that camper mattresses are commonly thin and poorly supported—most are only about 4 inches thick. That can make for a less-than-satisfying slumber.

Side-by-side bunks are a great option if your camper will involve friends or family who would prefer not to share a bed.

But never fear: you can cover any camper mattress with an inexpensive aftermarket foam topper that will make the bed much more comfortable, and many manufacturers make more luxurious replacement mattresses for campers. The less flexible issue is the actual size of the bed. The only way to see whether you'll be able to sleep comfortably in the bed of the camper you're checking out is to kick off your shoes and actually lie down. If you sleep with a partner, keep in mind limb sprawl and how much you both move during the night. More important is how hard or easy the bed is to get in and out of. Is there an overhead cabinet that you're going to rap your noggin on every time you get up to go to the bathroom? Is there enough legroom on each side of the bed to put on shoes or slippers? Is there enough of a lane of travel around the bed that getting in and out won't be a constant hassle?

WINDOWS

Open them. Are they easy to open or do they stick? Do they shut tight or do they allow airflow even when closed? Warping, rust, rot, cracks, and scratches are all signs that the window has seen better days. Windows can also be good barometers of the overall state of the camper's structure. If they are misaligned in their openings, or jam when being opened or closed, the trailer itself may have been exposed to significant torsional forces.

Rap on the glass lightly; some owners opt to replace broken windows with cheaper Plexiglas, which will eventually fog and deform. Also check closely around the window frame. This area is usually the first to experience water damage, and a key indicator that there may be leaks throughout the camper.

A bank of windows, such as the ones surrounding this glamper's dinette, can be a plus in an otherwise dark interior. It's also a chance to add decorative elements with fun and colorful window treatments.

If you do find damaged windows, they shouldn't necessarily knock that candidate off your list. Many manufacturers make replacement windows, including specific windows for older models and even hard-to-find versions such as jalousie windows. They are also easy and quick to replace, and require no special skill.

STEREOS AND ENTERTAINMENT SYSTEM

It's a sad truth that RV sound systems are notoriously bad. If you're considering an older camper, chances are that won't be a problem because there's probably no stereo system to worry about (and you can easily retrofit a system that meets your budget and listening requirements in equal measure). If there is a sound system, turn it on with the doors closed and listen to talk radio and different types of music. Does the music reach where you'll be spending most of your time in the camper? If there are external speakers, check them out by standing outside at different distances from the trailer. You'll also need to consider the music source. Do you listen to radio mostly, or are you dedicated to your music player? Still have an impressive CD collection? Make sure the sound system will play your music in the format you most often use.

QUICK TIP

Before plunking down that massive check to buy your 40-foot dream land yacht, consider where your travels will take you. Many state parks and campgrounds limit the length of trailer they'll allow—many cap trailer length at 28 feet.

THE GREAT BIG, ALL-ENCOMPASSING CAMPER INSPECTION CHECKLIST

So you've made your pick and you can envision many a happy lakeside weekend in your new-old travel trailer or truck camper. Now all you have do is write that check and drive away a truly "happy camper."

Not so fast. Before you buy any camper, you absolutely must inspect it—or have it inspected. You can use a local RV dealership to do this, but the logistics and expense (especially if you wind up deciding against the purchase) make this an easy and wise do-it-yourself option. It's also a way to get more familiar with a structure you'll hopefully be maintaining and enjoying.

A thorough inspection is your protection against buying a trailer that is better scrapped than towed. Given that thousands of dollars may be at stake, it's an hour or so of your time and effort well spent.

The number-one issue of concern in buying a used camper of any type is water damage. Water is the worst enemy of a camper's systems and structure. That's why you'll be looking for any signs of water infiltration, rot, or mold, no matter which part of the camper you're inspecting. This means using your eyes, as well as your nose and your sense of touch.

WHAT YOU'LL NEED

- ☐ Work gloves
- ☐ Eye and ear protection
- ☐ Stepladder
- ☐ Awl or probe
- ☐ Screwdriver
- ☐ Flashlight
- ☐ Measuring tape
- ☐ Notepad and pencil
- ☐ Rag

START WITH THE OUTSIDE.

Scan up and down the walls, moving from one side to the other. Check for obvious damage or defects. Specifically, look for separation (the outside panel pulling away from the underlying bonding surface) in fiberglass siding. No matter what type of siding the camper boasts, if a section flexes when you press on it, that's a bad sign—evidence of potential large-scale rot. Other damage you should note:

- Dents? How big and where? (Assess whether panel replacement or repair will be necessary.) Dings that are just aesthetic do not need to be immediately remedied, if ever.

- Missing screws in panels? (Potential water infiltration; check on the inside at those points.)

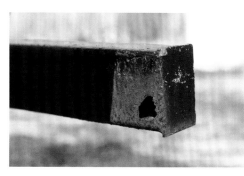

Small bits of rust are just a cosmetic issue, but larger areas on the body of a camper can indicate problems with leaks.

- Rust? (Small spots are rarely a problem; larger areas point to neglect and potential water problems.)

- Softness when you press wall panels? (Fiberglass delamination and/or compromised underlying structure due to damage or water infiltration.)

CAREFULLY PRY AWAY EXTERIOR CORNER TRIM AND SEAL (IF ANY).

- Are screw heads rusted over? (The seal has failed and water has made it under the trim and possibly into the substructure.)

- Visible moisture in corner channels?

- Corner bead/trim missing or damaged? (Urgent repair situation; water can easily infiltrate these areas.)

INSPECT AROUND WINDOWS AND DOORS.

- Are seals missing, or sections of seals or caulking beads missing?

- Are there any unusually large gaps? (Torsional forces may have bent the tow frame or damaged the structure.)

- Door or window misaligned in its opening? (May need to be replaced—especially misaligned windows.)

- Opens smoothly and easily? Locks securely?

- Are there scratches, cracks, or chips in the windows? Separation between glass and frame? (Indicates possibly costly window replacement, depending on how unusual the window shape and size are.)

- Is the weather stripping around the door intact? (Could be a sign of poor maintenance on the part of the previous owner.)

NOW IT'S LADDER TIME.

Any camper's roof—if in satisfactory condition—should easily support your weight. Still, step carefully and try to step only on trusses or rafters, and use lightweight shoes with rubber or similar soles.

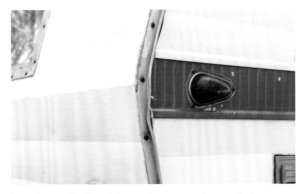

Rusted screw heads and damaged seams can be a particular warning of water infiltration.

Is the door off in its alignment with the frame?

- Check for soft areas. The roof should be rigid. (A lot of give in any one area indicates water infiltration and rot. Note the location for when you inspect the inside of the camper.)

- Closely check seals or caulking around projections such as air-conditioning units and vents. Are seals or caulking deteriorating, peeling, or missing? (Cleaning and replacing seals and caulking is a part of regular maintenance that is often overlooked and often done wrong. Can indicate poor overall maintenance.)

Are there soft areas or deteriorating seals on the roof?

- Are all vent caps in place and secure? Is there any damage to the A/C hood or other rooftop fixtures? (Could be a sign of poor towing practices that might indicate other damage elsewhere, such as in the suspension.)

- Are there any tears, punctures, or other apparent defects in a rubber roof? (Can point to the need for rubber roof replacement.)

UNDERNEATH THE CAMPER.

Put on a pair of safety glasses, grab your flashlight, and make your way underneath the camper to inspect the tow frame and undercarriage. (Obviously, if you're considering a truck camper, you get to stay a little cleaner and skip this part.)

- Are there obvious signs of damage to the frame: large dents, creases, or deep scratches?

- Are all the welds intact, with no apparent fractures or fissures? Are there any newer welds? (Can indicate serious damage and attempted repair.)

- Does the frame appear twisted, uneven, or otherwise misaligned?

- Is there any contact damage, cracking, or other deformity in the axle? (Indicates off-road abuse and can be an expensive repair waiting to happen.)

- Are the axle brackets secure and undamaged? (These are a common failure point for the suspension.)

- Are the springs/shocks intact, free of cracks or other damage?

- Are there any soft spots/areas of rot when you probe the subfloor?

- Water stains or other signs of water or rot infiltration?

CHECK THE HITCH AND PROPANE HOOKUPS.

Inspect the tanks closely, all the way around and on the bottom.

- Are the propane tanks dented, rusted, or otherwise damaged? (A new propane tank can run more than $100.)

- Date on the propane tanks? Are they close to needing recertification? (Tanks must be recertified after twelve years.)

- Disconnect the regulator and look at it closely. Is there a black fluid leaking out? (A sign that the regulator needs to be replaced.)

- Are the hookup fittings on the regulator, pressure gauge, solenoid, and pigtails secure and undamaged?

- Are the hoses intact, pliable, and free of cracks?

- Is there a propane tank cover? Is it free of cracks or damage? (Tanks deteriorate much more quickly when exposed to the elements and road debris.)

TIRES AND BRAKES.

To thoroughly check the tires and brakes, you'll need to jack up one side of the trailer and remove a tire. This is a dirty process and you should keep rags on hand. If this seems like too much hassle, keep in mind that a blowout while driving can be a catastrophic event. Don't let their small size fool you; camper tires are vitally important, and it's essential to know the state of the tires and brakes on any camper you're considering buying.

Remove the tire and set aside, being careful to place the lug nuts in a secure place. Use a screwdriver to pry off the dust cap, and then use pliers to remove the cotter pin. Pull out the bearings and remove the drum.

- Clean and check the bearings. Is there any apparent damage, or play in the bearing rollers? (Damaged bearings can be an indication of sloppy maintenance.)

- Measure the brake pad linings. Is there more than $1/10$" remaining on each shoe? (If not, the brakes will need to be replaced immediately.)

- Are the drum springs in good shape?

- Is the magnet still active? (See whether the pliers stick to it.)

- Connect to a tow vehicle and test the brakes by having a helper step on the brakes. Do the brakes activate?

- Look closely at the inner and outer sidewalls of the tires.

- Is there apparent cracking or bulging?

- Are the tires underinflated?

- Are they marked "ST"? (The correct designation for camper trailer tires.)

- Is the tread overly worn?

Replace the brake drum and bearings, tighten and back off the lock nut, insert a new cotter pin, and reinstall the cap. Replace the tire.

ON THE LEVEL

It's important that camper trailers be kept level. It's not just a matter of comfort—sleeping without rolling out of the bed, or having your silverware not slide off the dinette table. It's also essential to refrigerator function and proper distribution of weight across the entire structure. Different camper trailers employ different leveling systems. These are often overlooked by the first-time camper buyer, but it's essential to check leveling features prior to purchase.

Truck campers usually rely on the simplest type of leveling: planks under the truck's tires. Many truck camper owners keep a simple bubble level in the cab and look to park in fairly level campsite spaces. You'll still want to check the function and integrity of the telescoping jacks at the front of the camper, which support it when it's not in the bed of the truck. They should slide out smoothly and securely lock in place when extended.

Teardrops and pop-up campers are often supported by independent front and back scissor jacks (not a part of the camper structure). On older units, leveling is a manual process—there are often bubble levels built right into the sides of the camper body. Newer or higher end units usually feature electrically powered hydraulic jacks that make leveling much easier.

The more complex jacks built into travel trailers and fifth wheels make leveling these trailers easier, but they are also subject to more problems. Basic crank jacks are uncomplicated and work or don't, but something like screw-type posts that are lowered and raised with a power drill equipped with a special bit can experience several different malfunctions.

MOVING INSIDE.

You'll want to check the systems for proper function, and the space itself for signs of damage or defect. That means trying out all the appliances, which will require powering up the trailer. Inspecting the inside of a camper also means using your sense of smell.

- Light all burners on a cooktop and adjust the flame to different heights (or heat the burners of an electric cooktop). Are there any dead spots in the burners? Are there any other malfunctions that point to possible cooktop replacement?

- Is the refrigerator in good working order and has it cooled down to an appropriate temperature?

- Check the hot water heater's anode rod. Is the rod due for replacement? (Some older RV water heaters did not come equipped with an anode rod.)

- Does the toilet flush as it should?

- Is there enough room for you in the shower/wet room?

The most convenient system features hydraulic jacks lowered and leveled from a control panel. Any of these should be checked through the actual process of raising, lowering, and leveling. Telescoping posts are prone to road damage, improper storage, and the occasional ding from obstacles. Whether manual or hydraulic, the post should telescope and retract smoothly and completely. Post receivers should be firmly attached to the camper and show no obvious signs of damage or separation that would allow for water infiltration.

- Are the seams in the bathroom intact? Any sign of mold, including a musty smell?
- Does the bathroom fan seem to be pulling strongly?

HEATING AND COOLING.

Depending on the type of camping you'll be doing, heating and cooling may be crucial. The only way to adequately test those features is to run them with the doors and windows closed. No matter what you find out, remember that in most cases, air conditioners and furnaces can be upgraded or retrofit into vintage campers that lack them.

- Does the air conditioner cool down the camper in a reasonable amount of time?
- Check the thermostat. Can the air conditioner cool the interior temperature to 70 degrees while not on the maximum setting? (RV air conditioners are notoriously underpowered, and weaken with age.)
- Are there any hot spots that stay noticeably warmer than the rest of the interior?

- Is the air conditioner unusually loud? (A sign of possible impending breakdown.)

- Does the furnace heat the entire camper quickly?

STORAGE AREAS.

Cabinets and closets can be even more revealing about the general structural integrity of the camper overall. You should open every storage area.

- Any mildew smell?

- Do you see signs of black mold? Can you feel heat coming from a cabinet or closet with signs of mold? (A sign that the mold has been there for quite some time and the colony is flourishing.)

- Is there give or softness when you press on the inside walls of a cabinet or closet?

- Any soft spots on the floor, or cracking in the flooring?

- Are there any visible water stains?

FURNISHINGS.

Although systems are more complex, furnishings become important over time because they determine just how comfortable any given camping trip will be.

- Is the bed comfortable and large enough for you to sleep comfortably?

- Can you easily move around the bed—say, to make it each morning?

- Are you able to sit up in bed without hitting your head on overhead cabinets or other objects?

- Are there bedside lights?

- Can you get in and out of the dinette easily?

- Are the dinette benches and other seating in the main cabin comfortable, or would they give you a back or neck ache after sitting for long periods (such as reading a newspaper or book)?

- Are there any signs of vermin (feces) under the cushions?

GETTING A FAIR PRICE

When shopping for a used camper, it's good to have some idea what a "reasonable" price really is. NADAguides for RVs (www.nadaguides.com/RVs) is essentially a Blue Book for camper trailers of all kinds.

The actual worth of a used camper depends on a lot of variables. The area of the country you live in, the number of similar models on the market, and the desirability of the particular camper may all affect what price might be considered reasonable. Certain key add-ons, like a power slide-out or a large, luxury refrigerator, will add hundreds if not more than a thousand dollars to the value. You're not likely to find much variation in the market with older campers, but from about the mid-1970s on, the type and number of options exploded; the difference between a stripped-down bare 1984 truck camper and a fully loaded version with the highest-end options can be more than $2,000 in resale price.

THE DEAL BREAKERS

Some damage and signs of camper deterioration are simply terminal; fixing them would require as much or more expense as the unit's worth, or the problem can't be satisfactorily remedied. If you see these signs—no matter how much you love that 1964 canned ham—run.

- **PERVASIVE ROT.** If you're noticing sections of rot on both the roof and the floor, the water damage is extensive and has most likely compromised the integrity of the entire camper's structure.

- **MOLD INFILTRATION.** Uncovered several areas of black growth? A moisture problem has persisted for so long that it has fostered colonies of unhealthy and potentially toxic mold. Do you feel heat coming from a mold-infected cabinet or closet, and find multiple areas of mold in the same trailer? Don't risk your health and your investment.

- **COMPROMISED TOW FRAME.** If you find significant cracks, broken welds, or areas of impact damage where the frame has actually bent, you're better off continuing your search for a camper. It's not just the expense of repairs; when the tow frame has been damaged this severely, chances are that the rest of the trailer has absorbed some of that damage as well.

- **FIBERGLASS DELAMINATION.** If large sections of fiberglass sidewall or roof seem to flex loosely, the siding has separated from the substrate. The problem will only get worse with time and travel, and the repairs are extremely costly. It's wiser to look for another camper.

- **MULTIPLE FIXTURES AND OUTLETS WITHOUT POWER.** This is possible evidence that the owner has tried to deal with an electrical problem and made it worse. The trailer could present a fire hazard, and doesn't represent a bargain at any price.

THE NEW RETRO

Dig a retro look but not into doing all the work necessary to resuscitate an old road warrior to its past glory? No problem. Turn to the handful of manufacturers that are producing brand-new trailers in vintage styles. These companies are combining modern materials and technology in looks and floor plans from yesteryear, or their own spins on what retro should look like.

One of CH Campers' retro-styled trailers.

- **CH CAMPERS.** CH re-creates the vintage canned ham look in a small line of modern trailers that are as comfortable as they are full of flair. They offer a limited product line as well as building to suit a customer's preference. Their trailers include wet rooms, fridges, and cooktops, and can even be equipped with air conditioners. The company also offers reproduction parts for those individuals who have decided to build their own timeless camper. (www.chcamper.com)

- **DUB-BOX-USA.** This unique company produces trailers that look like a classic VW Camper Van without the front wheels. The campers are constructed with a fiberglass shell, making them lightweight. The interiors are full of style and comfortable and you have options—sinks, cooktops, and air-conditioning. (www.dub-box-usa.com)

- **HAPPIER CAMPER.** It may look old, but this egg-shaped trailer is cutting edge. Happier Camper produces super basic ultralight trailers with bonded fiberglass shells and "modular" interior elements that allow for a great deal of customization. The trailers include solar panels, Bose speakers, and a tiny size that easily fits anywhere and is a dream to tow. But be aware, you won't find a kitchen or bathroom in these modest marvels—they're basically for sleeping out in style. (www.happiercamper.com)

- **SERRO SCOTTY.** One of the most beloved trailers of the '60s, the Serro Scotty travel trailer has been brought back to life by Little Guy Trailers, in five 14-foot to 21-foot models. The trailers include all the amenities you would expect, including full bathrooms, cooktops, and comfortable sleeping quarters. (www.serroscottytrailers.com)

Dub-Box-USA trailer, inside and out.

- **T@B TEARDROPS.** These are not, strictly speaking, re-creations of a bygone brand. But the teardrop trailers that T@B produces certainly capture the style and panache of mid-century standouts. Boldly colored, these are large teardrops, including some models that feature both kitchens and bathrooms in compact, well-designed layouts. (www.tab-rv.com)

- **BOWLUS ROAD CHIEF.** This luxury travel trailer comes in two models and is entirely evocative of camping's golden age. With a polished aluminum skin, spacious and well-appointed interior, and a streamlined "arrow" shape, the Bowlus captures everything you might want in a high-end vintage camper, but with brand-new construction and modern durability and technology. (www.bowlusroadchief.com)

2

CAMPER EXTERIORS

The outside of that lovely camper trailer you've just brought home is where problems often start. Siding oxidizes, delaminates, or discolors in response to repeated weather exposure. Suspensions and hitches start to go wonky after one too many potholes, brake slams, or hard turns. The seals around doors and windows inevitably give up the ghost, and windows crack from an unexpectedly hard jolt or blow from a low-hanging tree branch. Rehabbing any camper can involve dealing with any or all of these issues, and even if they're not present at the time you buy a used trailer, they're likely to pop up sooner or later.

The oxidation making this aluminum trailer appear dull gray is not necessarily a terminal condition. It's normal and requires only a cleaning and polishing to preserve the skin. However, it will take considerably more work to get to the unparalleled look of a mirror finish.

SKIN CARE

A camper's skin endures a remarkable amount of abuse, which is why this area is the most common point of water infiltration and structural failure. Imagine how you'd look if you carted yourself down a thousand miles of road without sunscreen, an umbrella, or clothes to protect you from the blazing sun, and then slept naked outside in all kinds of weather when you got home.

It's not just punishment from the elements you have to worry about, either; camper cladding has to stay tight on the unit's skeleton while the structure flexes and responds to a bazillion rocks, potholes, road cracks, and speed bumps. On top of all that, there's the occasional inaccurate parking job that rams a low tree branch against the camper roof or side. And there are a wealth of seams and seals on any old camper into which water can easily seep.

The first line of defense and the first step in rehabbing are one and the same: a good cleaning.

Some pros recommend a thorough cleaning even before you buy a used camper, as a way to more clearly assess the state of the roof and siding in advance of writing a check. That seems a bit much, but a good cleaning should be number one on the to-do list when you get your new toy home. Keep in mind that, by using the right products in the right way, you might well be able to restore the finish on that aged Shasta trailer to what it looked like coming off the assembly line—even if it looks far gone and extremely oxidized on purchase. It's always worth your time to deep clean the camper before jumping into more serious options like sanding and repainting.

Washing a camper is not as simple as washing a car; it's easy to use the wrong cleaning and maintenance products, and you can actually degrade the skin and protective coatings. Make sure you avoid doing more harm than good by purchasing products explicitly labeled for your camper's siding material and following the instructions on the labels and any supplied by the camper's original manufacturer. Manufacturers provide recommendations for cleaning methods and acceptable chemicals and cleaners with their campers. But if you've landed that super-cool

A painted corrugated aluminum exterior is a classic look and easy to maintain, as long you regularly clean the surface and keep it free of dirt, grease, and road grime.

When it comes to cleaning your camper, only use products labeled for the specific materials you're cleaning. There are products on the market for cleaning and protecting every type of siding and roof, and even specialty products for specific areas, such as caulking and seals.

UNDER PRESSURE

Camper trailers are large. Go through the effort of washing one by hand and it can become awfully tempting to just blast dirt off with a pressure washer, but think twice about that. Pressure washing can damage thin aluminum or fiberglass siding, and even remove surface decals that form the designs on some smooth-sided campers. If you're looking to take this particular shortcut, it's always wise to consult the recommendations from the camper's manufacturer. If you must go the shock-and-awe method, though, follow these guidelines to avoid damage:

- Hold the spray head no closer than 3 feet from the surface.

- Avoid using more than 2,500 psig.

- Ideally, use a 40-degree fan tip or wider.

- Spray downward from the roof of the trailer, and outward from doors, windows, vents, and any other openings.

- Do not spray directly into vent grills.

- Spray the undercarriage as part of the cleaning process.

If you own a particularly large fifth wheel, consider using the wash bay at a truck stop. They are specifically meant to accommodate large and tall semi-trailers.

canned ham trailer that's older than you are, chances are the manufacturer's instructions—and maybe the manufacturer itself—are just a memory. So here are some guidelines, just in case.

Special cleaners are available for specific types of dirt and debris, such as road tar, bugs, and the detritus that normally sheds from rubber roofs. Again, check the label to ensure the cleaner is appropriate for the siding on your camper. When in doubt, always test on an inconspicuous area.

Clean your camper on an overcast day when the skin is cool to the touch, and use the right equipment: a telescoping wash brush (not a push broom), a microfiber chamois, a soft hand brush, and a large bucket. Before cleaning, always close vents, windows, and doors. Begin by thoroughly wetting the surface down.

FIBERGLASS

There are two types of fiberglass camper skins: gel coat and painted. Gel-coated pigment is applied during manufacturing and is integral to the surface. Regardless of the type, use a cleaner meant specifically for synthetic surfaces. There are actually a range of products used on fiberglass RVs and boats, each with its own strengths and weaknesses. Some can be pricey, but don't let thrift guide your decision. The longevity of your camper's skin will usually provide a good return on investment.

Whatever products you choose, avoid abrasive cleaners, which can damage a protective gel coat. Fiberglass camper skins should also be waxed at least twice a year to prevent degradation from sun exposure.

- **CLEANER.** Shop for cleaners labeled specifically for use on fiberglass boats and RVs. Start with those meant for issues like the black and white streaks naturally produced by a rubber roof, and then pick up a general, all-purpose cleaner. Read labels carefully before using the product.

- **POLISHER.** Polishers require a lot of elbow grease even if you're using a rotary polisher with wool pads. But these products can bring an older fiberglass skin back to life. Used correctly, a polisher will remove all traces of oxidation and give the surface an unrivaled glossy shine. Polishing a fiberglass skin is immediately followed by waxing to ensure that the surface is protected from sunlight and other exposure.

- **CLEANER-WAX.** This combo product can reduce the amount of work you need to do and is good at removing common oxidation. However, experts believe that these products are usually somewhat less effective than the two products used separately.

- **WAX.** You'll find many natural waxes—made from substances like beeswax—that are safe and effective to use on fiberglass surfaces. However, for maximum protection, it's usually wisest to select a synthetic polymer sealant, which will provide stronger, longer-lasting protection from sun and weather.

HOW TO REPAIR DAMAGED FIBERGLASS SIDING

All it takes is a simple misjudgment in backing your trailer into a narrow campsite space and, boom, you have a nice crack or hole in your camper's fiberglass skin. Obviously, any rupture has to be remedied as soon as possible to prevent water infiltration. Fortunately, you won't need a body shop's worth of skills and tools to make the repair. But you should work slowly and carefully to fully blend the patch area into the side or roof of the camper. Take your time and nobody will know that there was ever any damage to the skin.

WHAT YOU'LL NEED

- ☐ Work gloves
- ☐ Eye and ear protection
- ☐ Cleaner
- ☐ Heavy-duty shears
- ☐ Dust mask
- ☐ Sanding block
- ☐ Disposable latex gloves
- ☐ Fiberglass patch kit, including two-part resin and fiberglass cloth
- ☐ Measuring tape
- ☐ Paintbrush
- ☐ Roller
- ☐ Fiberglass body filler and hardener
- ☐ Wood or plastic fid
- ☐ Small square of cardboard
- ☐ Plastic sheeting
- ☐ Painter's tape or masking tape
- ☐ Paint
- ☐ Paint gun

1 Clean the area to remove any dirt or grease. With heavy-duty shears, cut away jagged ends and any loose, broken pieces in the dent area. Gently pull out the damaged section to make it as flush as possible with the rest of the surface. Wearing a dust mask, sand the edges of the damaged area, feathering out all around the damage.

2 Mix the fiberglass patch resin according to the manufacturer's instructions. Measure for the patch and cut the fiberglass cloth to match the dimensions. Cut a second patch to match the first.

3 Wearing latex gloves, brush resin over the patch area. Lightly soak the patch in the resin, and then apply it over the damaged area. Smooth it with a roller until it's entirely secured to the surface, flat, and free of bubbles. Let the resin cure for the time recommended by the manufacturer.

4 Mix the body filler with the hardener, blending them with a fid, on a small square of cardboard. Once the filler is completely blended with the hardener, use the fid to press the filler over the patch area. Smooth it as much as possible to avoid extra sanding. Let the body filler dry completely.

5 Sand the area to feather the patch into the surrounding siding. You may need to apply additional coats of body filler, sanding after each, until the surface is perfectly smooth and level. Sand one last time with 180-grit sandpaper.

6 Isolate the area to be painted with plastic sheet and masking tape or painter's tape. Leave enough area around the patch area to convincingly blend the paint into the rest of the siding. Match the paint to the existing siding color (if you can't match exactly, you'll need to repaint the entire camper). Use an electric or compressed-air paint sprayer to lay down several very light coats, sanding between each, and feathering the paint at the edges into the larger surface.

SHAPED PAINTED ALUMINUM SIDING

Like fiberglass skin, older painted aluminum camper siding can be revitalized with a number of products used separately or in tandem. The key is to use the products in the correct order. No matter which product you choose, the enemy is oxidation. Never fear, though: something like a "finish restorer" used in conjunction with a general cleaner can give older aluminum vibrant new life.

- **RESTORER.** These are formulated to remove the oxidation common to vintage aluminum campers, along with a micro-thin layer of the old paint. By doing that, the product reveals the unprotected base coat in its original color and sheen. Restorers take a lot of effort and time, but the results can be transformative. Most are meant to be used before cleaning, although some are used after the surface has been cleaned and dried. As always, check the label.

- **SPECIALIZED STAIN TREATMENTS.** Turn to RV supply stores and marine product outlets for cleaners meant to deal with particular stains—from mold, to tar, to leaf stains. These are used before a general cleaner.

- **CLEANER.** A cleaner formulated for use on painted aluminum siding—such as cleaners meant for painted aluminum house siding—can work wonders, but you need to follow the manufacturer's instructions precisely for best results.

- **WAX, SEALER, OR PROTECTANT.** All three of these products provide lasting protection against UV and other degradation. The difference is in the amount of protection. Wax can make painted aluminum look like new, but offers the least amount of protection. Sealers and protectants are stronger and longer lasting. All three of these are also combined with cleaners in all-in-one products.

QUICK TIP

The icing on the cake of a freshly washed camper is gleaming tire sidewalls. But pay attention to the products you use; many tire-polishing products contain alcohol or petroleum distillates that can dry the rubber out and lead to sidewall cracking and early deterioration.

A corrugated aluminum skin such as this is fairly easy to keep in good shape and looking its best. All you'll need is a general aluminum cleaner, and perhaps a restorer product to remove built-up oxidation.

HOW TO REPAINT A VINTAGE ALUMINUM CAMPER

There are a couple of ways to paint an aluminum-sided camper. Although you could use a paintbrush and roller, the most efficient, and the way most likely to result in a beautiful, factory-quality paint job, is with a compressor-powered air sprayer. No matter what, the underlying surface must be spotlessly clean and prepped. This usually means sanding down rough spots or bad areas, but you can also strip the siding if the paint is compromised all over.

1 Thoroughly wash the surface, using a degreasing cleaner meant for use on aluminum. Be careful to remove all road grime, stains, and grease. Dry with clean, lint-free towels.

> **NOTE:** If there is an abundance of loose paint, you can remove much of it with a power washer—but see the note on page 68 about the risks of using a power washer on your camper.

WHAT YOU'LL NEED

- ☐ Work gloves
- ☐ Eye and ear protection
- ☐ Degreasing cleaner for aluminum
- ☐ Clean, lint-free towels
- ☐ Masking tape
- ☐ 6-mil plastic sheeting or plastic painter's drop cloth

- ☐ Dust mask
- ☐ Power drill with wire wheel
- ☐ Electric spray gun or air-powered spray gun
- ☐ Primer and paint (labeled for use on aluminum)
- ☐ Sanding block
- ☐ Tack cloth

2 Either mask off and tape over or remove the windows, entry and storage doors, taillights, cover plates, and trim. Mask and tape off any areas that shouldn't be painted and can't easily be removed, such as the wheels.

3 Wearing a dust mask, use a power drill fitted with a wire wheel attachment to clean up the surface of the camper, removing loose paint and smoothing out any rough areas (i.e., stickers or other decorative elements). Make sure the area you'll be painting in is blocked from wind, has good ventilation, and is free of dust and debris that might ruin the paint job.

NOTE: *If the trailer has already had multiple paint jobs, you may need to take the finish down to bare metal. This is a big job and requires an "airplane" paint stripper. Follow the manufacturer's directions.*

4 Use an electric spray rig and high-quality gun or a compressed air gun (it's usually wisest to rent the rig, because the cost of a professional spray gun is prohibitive) to lay down a coat of primer. Spray side to side, working from the top down. Do one entire side before moving on to the next. Start with a coat of primer meant specifically for aluminum.

5 Let the primer dry entirely, usually at least 24 hours. Sand any areas that are still rough with a fine-grit sanding block. Clean up any dust with a tack cloth. Tape off areas to be painted different colors. Paint the topmost stripes or patterns first, moving to lower sections after the top has been allowed to dry.

6 When the top coat has completely cured (check the manufacturer's instructions for drying and curing time), replace any fixtures or windows you've removed and strip off all tape and masking, being careful not to scratch the new paint during the process. Reapply caulking or seals as necessary.

POLISHED ALUMINUM

There's nothing quite like the long oval shape and shine of a polished aluminum trailer. Lovely as it is, that look takes a fair bit of care to maintain. The biggest enemy is oxidation, which shows itself as a dull gray film. But bird poop, sun exposure, and other contaminants don't help the appearance either. For best results, wash your polished aluminum trailer once a month, following these rules.

Gently prewash the exterior with a soft stream of conditioned (soft) water, starting at the top and working down. Wash with the "grain" of the aluminum, using a soft washing mitt or soft bristle brush. Wash with a cleaner formulated specifically for unpainted aluminum surfaces (you'll need to determine whether your camper's surface is coated or uncoated aluminum). The best formulas combine cleaning, polishing, and glazing actions.

Always clean off road grime, sap, and similar dirt immediately after a trip, because it will be easier to remove when it's fresh. Even stubborn tar can be removed with a soft cloth moistened with kerosene or turpentine. Remove water spots whenever you detect them with a soft cloth moistened with a 1:1 mixture of water and vinegar.

Regardless of your camper's siding, your regular washing ritual should include cleaning and conditioning seals, gaskets, and caulking. This means treating the areas around rooftop fixtures and openings, side holes meant for air conditioners, and slide-out room gaskets.

Choose a cleaner-conditioner meant for the material or the gasket or seal. Usually, this means either a product formulated for rubber (modern slide-out seals and rubber roof seals and gaskets) or silicone (beads around fixtures on metal or fiberglass roofs). You may not necessarily need to buy a cleaning and conditioning product. For instance, baby powder is often used to keep rubber gaskets and seals in like-new condition. Regularly coat the seal with the powder by sprinkling it on a clean, lint-free cloth and rubbing it into the seal. Check your owner's manual for other suggestions from the manufacturer.

Maintaining a mirror polish on an aluminum trailer begins with a thorough cleaning.

HOW TO POLISH ALUMINUM SKIN

A good washing and waxing are all that's needed to turn painted aluminum and fiberglass vintage campers into driveway trophies. But when it comes to bare aluminum siding, the key to a truly stunning and classic look is regular repolishing. Be prepared: polishing even a small travel trailer takes a lot of time and hard work. But the proud owners of Airstreams and other polished aluminum campers usually feel that the results are well worth the effort, especially at the moment when they step back and see their funhouse-mirror reflection in the side of their classic camper.

WHAT YOU'LL NEED

- ☐ Work gloves
- ☐ Eye and ear protection
- ☐ Plastic sheeting
- ☐ Painter's tape
- ☐ Clean, lint-free cloths

- ☐ Toothpaste
- ☐ Paintbrush or paint sprayer
- ☐ Clear coat stripper (optional)
- ☐ Power washer
- ☐ Coarse, nonabrasive aluminum polish

- ☐ 7" orbital polisher and wool pads
- ☐ Medium abrasive aluminum polish
- ☐ Random orbital dual-pad polisher with bonnets (optional)
- ☐ Finish product (optional)

1 Wash the surface. Clean the trailer as described on page 73, then protect what you won't be polishing with plastic sheet and painter's tape. Light lenses and plastic or painted parts should be removed or taped off.

2 Remove any protectant layer. Many aluminum trailers are treated with a clear protective coating generically called "clear coat." It must be removed prior to polishing. (Check for the coating by lightly scrubbing a clean, out-of-sight area with a white, lint-free cloth dabbed with white toothpaste. If the cloth comes away black after rubbing the surface, there is no clear coat layer. Check several areas of the trailer to be sure.) Brush or spray a clear-coat removal product over the skin on a cool, overcast day, or after the sun goes down. Always follow the manufacturer's instructions and safety precautions.

3 Wait several hours or overnight, and then use a power washer on its lowest setting to spray off the material and the clear coat. The clear coat will come off in visible pieces and sections.

4 Polish off any oxidation using a coarse, nonabrasive polish meant for oxidized metal, and a 7-inch or larger orbital polisher fit with a hook-and-loop pad. Work in areas about 3-foot square. Dab small dollops of polish every 6 inches across the square. Be modest with the amount of polish, because too much polish will make for more work and a less effective process.

5 The polisher should be on a slow speed for this step. Hold the pad at a 30-degree angle to the surface, and keep it moving. Make multiple passes, alternating side to side, then up and down. Polish until all traces of residue, scratches, and marks are removed.

NOTE: This step is only necessary if the trailer has not been polished in the previous year.

6 Once you've finished polishing the entire surface with the primary polish (usually starting with "F" grade), move onto the medium abrasive "C" polish. Fit a new pad onto the orbital polisher. Polish the surface using the same procedure you did with the coarse abrasive polish.

7 Although some camper owners finish with a "C" polish, if you want a true "mirror" finish, you'll need to do one more stage with an "S" polish. Professionals use a random orbital dual-head polisher. The polisher requires polishing bonnets that can run to a considerable expense. Most home craftsmen finish with the same orbital polisher and a new pad, using the same process as before, but moving the polisher in a more random pattern.

ROOFS

A roof over your head when camping is usually the very reason you buy a camper in the first place. But that roof is problematic; it's the area most susceptible to deterioration and damage. Although rubber roofs are the most common, your camper may be topped in aluminum or fiberglass. No matter what the surface is made of, you should regularly inspect it for potential leaks. That inspection should focus on seams, seals, and caulking around the various openings in the roof.

HOW TO RECAULK CAMPER SEALS AND SEAMS

1 Wash the camper thoroughly and let it dry. Inspect all the caulking, seams, and seals around windows and doors, and rooftop fixtures such as air-conditioning units, vents, and ladder mounts.

2 Use a utility knife to carefully cut away old, degraded caulking. Work slowly to avoid cutting siding or the roof.

3 Clean up the joints and other areas where you've removed caulking by scrubbing with a stiff-bristle brush, then use a rag and denatured alcohol to remove any remaining debris. Ensure that the surface is dry before proceeding.

4 Load a tube of the correct caulk for the material you're covering into a caulk gun. Cut a small opening at the end of the tube for more control. Lay a bead of caulk along the seam or seal area. Smooth it with your finger.

WHAT YOU'LL NEED

☐ Work gloves

☐ Eye and ear protection

☐ Utility knife

☐ Stiff bristle brush

☐ Denatured alcohol

☐ Clean rag

☐ Tube of caulk

☐ Caulk gun

HOW TO RECOAT A RUBBER ROOF

If you've bought a camper with a rubber roof, you can expect the roof to last a little more than a decade. Past that, you're camping on borrowed time. But there is a way to extend the life of a rubber EPDM roof. The roof can be recoated when it begins to look tired, stained, and worn—or every few years on a schedule, if you prefer. Recoating adds years to any rubber roof and is relatively easy. Figure about 1 gallon of coating compound per 100 square feet of roof.

1 Working on an overcast day (or in a shaded workspace), thoroughly clean the roof. Start by taping off the sides, front, and back of the trailer with painter's tape and plastic sheeting.

2 Use a broom to brush off any leaves or dry debris. Treat the entire roof with a rubber roof cleaner-activator, wearing a dust mask and latex gloves. Follow the manufacturer's instructions and either spread the cleaner with a roller or by spraying with a sprayer.

3 Leave the cleaner on the roof for 15 to 30 minutes, following the manufacturer's recommendations. Scrub down the roof with a medium-bristle wash brush and clean water, working in small areas to totally remove the cleaner. Rinse one final time with a hose fit with a spray nozzle.

NOTE: *As an alternative, clean the roof with a power washer set on low and the nozzle held 1 foot from the surface of the roof.*

4 Book a couple gallon cans into a 5-gallon bucket. Use a drill equipped with a paddle mixer on slow speed to mix the coating. If you're working with a two-part product, create a whirlpool with the paddle mixer and slowly pour in the catalyst. Follow the instructions on the can if they differ from these directions.

WHAT YOU'LL NEED

- ☐ Work gloves
- ☐ Eye and ear protection
- ☐ Painter's tape
- ☐ 6-mil plastic sheeting
- ☐ Rubber roof cleaner-activator
- ☐ Dust mask
- ☐ Latex gloves
- ☐ Paint roller or sprayer
- ☐ Telescoping medium-bristle wash brush
- ☐ Rubber roof coating
- ☐ Clean 5-gallon bucket
- ☐ Power drill and paddle mixer
- ☐ Clean 1- or 2-gallon plastic bucket
- ☐ 3" paintbrush
- ☐ Squeegee
- ☐ Medium-nap roller sleeve

5 Transfer some of the mix into a clean 1- or 2-gallon plastic bucket. Use this with a brush to lay down a wide band of the rubber coating around the edges of the roof fixtures such as lights, vents, and air-conditioning units.

6 Working at the corner further from your means of exiting the roof, pour out a little of the mix and spread evenly over a 4 × 4-foot area with the squeegee. Whatever product you're using, roll out the resurfacing mixture with a medium-nap sleeve and long handle. Allow the first coat to dry to the touch, then roll out a second coat. Let the final coat cure for the recommended period before using the trailer or allowing the roof to get wet.

NOTE: Some products can just be rolled on without being spread by squeegee. Follow the manufacturer's recommendations.

TOW FRAME AND SUSPENSION

The tow frame is an easy thing to forget about. After all, most of it's hidden. But your tow frame—and especially the wheels, brakes, and suspension—require inspection on a regular basis to make sure that no matter where you decide to camp, the trailer gets you where you're going. (Obviously, the elements won't be an issue with a truck camper.)

Old tow frames are often speckled with rust and deteriorated paint. Although the tow frame undercarriage is largely hidden from sight underneath the body of the trailer, the tongue is highly visible and a timeworn appearance will steal from the beauty of your camper's siding.

Add a nice accent to a restored older trailer by sprucing up the tongue. Remove the propane tanks, tongue jack if any, and all hardware. Tape the electrical connection

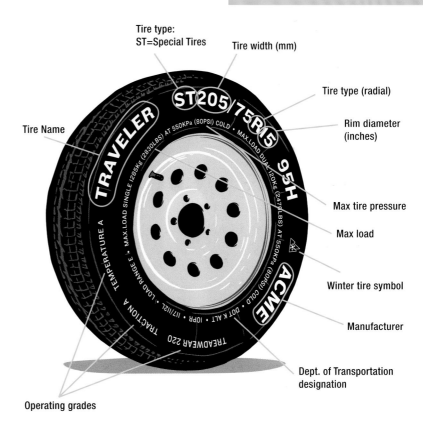

Tire type:
ST=Special Tires

Tire width (mm)

Tire type (radial)

Tire Name

Rim diameter (inches)

Max tire pressure

Max load

Winter tire symbol

Manufacturer

Dept. of Transportation designation

Operating grades

harness to the body of the camper. Use a wire wheel attachment on a power drill to clean up areas of rust and deteriorated paint (work on the undercarriage as well, to ensure long-term protection against dirt and water).

Prime the tongue and undercarriage with rust-resistant exterior metal primer. Let the primer dry fully and then apply a top coat of exterior enamel metal paint.

TIRES

A camper trailer's tires can seem insignificant, but don't be fooled. As the point of contact with the road, they are perhaps the most crucial part of any camper's suspension system. They must hold up in the face of bad roads, stresses from all directions, the weight of the camper above, and more. It's a lot to ask from what are essentially rubber-and-steel donuts. Fortunately, camper trailer tires are more than willing to spill the beans about their own readiness to hit the road and support your trailer. You just have to take the time to "read" them.

Start with the sidewall. Tires are, by law, embossed with their own biographical statistics. The writing is easy to decipher. See page 79.

Wear patterns can also tell you a lot about what is going on with not only the tire, but the suspension as well.

- **WEAR BARS.** If the wear bars that run across the tread are visible, the tire's tread has worn past allowable limits, and the tire should be replaced.

- **INSIDE EDGE WEAR.** This negative sign can indicate alignment issues, or overly worn ball joints or A-arm bushings.

WONDER WHEELS

You can dress up your vintage camper with a unique look by painting the tire rims. You don't even have to remove the tires from the rims to do it! Use a drill equipped with a wire wheel to strip the rim down to the metal, then wrap the tire securely in plastic. Lay the tire back-side down on a drop cloth, plastic sheet, or other protective surface. Spray the rim with a coat of rust-preventing primer. Let it dry, and spray the rims with a heavy-duty paint meant for metal, in your favorite color. Let the paint dry before removing the plastic. For the most stunning look, use a tire clean-and-shine product on the tires themselves.

- **OUTSIDE EDGE WEAR.** This is a symptom of any of the problems that cause inside edge wear, as well as a sign of underinflated tires.

- **CUPPING OR SCALLOPING.** This condition is caused by alignment, wheel, or suspension issues that require immediate attention.

- **SIDEWALL BULGING OR DEEP CRACKS.** Both are signs of impending tire failure and require the tires be replaced immediately.

The simplest and most effective technique for ensuring the integrity of your camper trailer's tires is to constantly check the inflation pressure. Always check tire pressure when the tire is cold and, at the very least, check the tires before every trip.

If you want to get the longest life out of your tires, cover them when the trailer is parked, so that the tires are not exposed to the sun's UV rays—a primary cause of tire deterioration.

BRAKES AND BRAKE SYSTEMS

Given how crucially important they are, even experienced DIYers can be leery of working on a camper trailer's brakes. That's understandable, but the actual brake assembly is fairly simple.

Most older campers feature basic drum brakes, so called because the brake shoes press outward on a drum that encloses the entire brake mechanism to stop the trailer. (Newer models have disk brakes, with shoes that squeeze down on a metal disk that is positioned parallel to the wheel.) The shoes are easy to replace by simply detaching the old shoes and replacing them with the new. You should always have the drum resurfaced when you replace the shoes, because over time, it wears unevenly due to imperfections in shoe pressure.

Although replacing brakes may well be something you prefer to leave to professionals, checking and servicing the wheel bearings is an entirely manageable maintenance chore that anyone with even modest automotive skills can do. It's also an easy way to ensure the camper keeps rolling without any wheel-related troubles.

A simple bulb burnout is one of the most common—and easiest to fix—problems with any camper trailer brake system.

HOW TO REPACK CAMPER TRAILER WHEEL BEARINGS

Although the tools you'll need to repack your trailer's wheel bearings may sound unfamiliar and will probably not be in your toolbox to start with, they are all inexpensive and widely available at automotive part stores, on the internet, and at some hardware stores. Fortunately, they are all incredibly easy to use as well.

The trick to packing wheel bearings is lots and lots of rags. The grease has a tendency to get everywhere, and the best job entails removing all the old grease that will have picked up a lot of dirt, debris, and microscopic metal fragments. Get on top of the grease situation, and the project should take you no more than a couple of hours front to back. Don't forget to inspect your brakes and your tires, because you're already taking everything apart.

1 Jack up one side of the trailer and remove the wheel. Pry the dust cap off with a standard screwdriver or slip-joint pliers. Use needle-nose pliers to straighten and pull out the cotter pin.

WHAT YOU'LL NEED

- ☐ Latex gloves
- ☐ Eye and ear protection
- ☐ Dust mask
- ☐ Jack
- ☐ Screwdriver
- ☐ Slip-joint pliers
- ☐ Needle-nose pliers
- ☐ Cardboard or clean newspaper
- ☐ Clean, lint-free rags
- ☐ Spray-on brake cleaner
- ☐ Seal puller (optional)

- ☐ Nylon or wood dowel (optional)
- ☐ Grease solvent
- ☐ Wheel-bearing grease (rated for use with wheel bearings)
- ☐ Bearing packer (optional)
- ☐ Grease seal
- ☐ Seal driver
- ☐ Ball-peen hammer
- ☐ Brake calipers
- ☐ Brake spoon
- ☐ Cotter pin

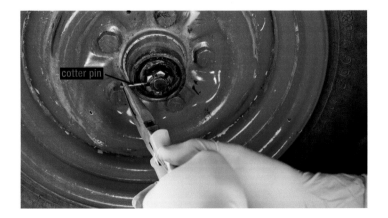

cotter pin

2 **TOP LEFT:** Unscrew the castle nut with the slip-joint pliers. Pull off the brake hub (or disk rotor) and set it back-side down on a separate square of cardboard or clean newspaper. The front bearing and washer should fall out into your hand as you pull the drum off the spindle.

3 **TOP RIGHT:** Inspect the brakes for damage, unusual wear, or other signs of defect indicating that the brakes should be replaced. Clean the spindle completely, either wiping it off or using spray-on brake cleaner if necessary.

4 **LEFT:** Remove the rear grease seal with a seal puller, or use a nylon or wood dowel and a mallet to knock the inner rear wheel bearings and grease seal out of the hub. Clean all the grease out of the drum hub's interior races.

5 **ABOVE:** Wash both sets of bearings in solvent until they are entirely clean. Check the bearings closely all over, turning each bearing to determine whether there are any defects such as chips, scratches, or discoloration (heat spots). Replace the bearings if there are obvious defects. Dry them with a clean, lint-free rag and let sit for an hour or more to ensure they are entirely free of any traces of solvent.

6 Repack the bearings with wheel-bearing grease. You can force grease in between bearings by pressing them into a dollop of grease held in the palm of your hand, or use a hydraulic packer (inexpensive and available at automotive supply stores). Slather grease on the inside ring and the outside of the bearings.

7 Regrease the inside of the hub. Put the inside bearing into place, and tap the grease seal over it with a seal driver.

> **NOTE:** *Although a seal driver is an inexpensive tool widely available at automotive supply stores, some home mechanics prefer to use a wood block. If you do this, seat the seal carefully, making sure it sits perfectly flush in the hub and hasn't deformed during installation.*

OPTIONAL: Technicians recommend calibrating drum brakes when you have the drum off, because trailer brakes are not self-adjusting. You'll need an inexpensive brake caliper. Hold the narrower arms to the inside of the drum, set the measurement, and place the opposite arms of the calipers over the brake shoes. Use a brake spoon or screwdriver to adjust the tensioner wheel on the back of the brake assembly.

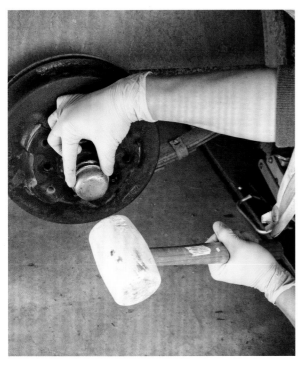

8 **TOP LEFT:** Lightly grease the spindle. Slide the hub back onto the spindle. Pack the outside bearings in the same way you did the inner bearings. Seat the bearings and slide the washer on top of the bearings.

9 **TOP RIGHT:** Screw the castle nut down until it's snug. Spin the drum to make sure it moves freely (there should be some resistance; it won't spin loosely). Back the castle nut off one-quarter of a turn.

10 **LEFT:** Slip a new cotter pin into place. Bend the ends flat against the castle nut. Slip the dust cap onto the end of the hub and lightly tap it to fully seat. Replace the tire and lower the trailer.

HITCH TYPES

The connection between your car or truck and your prized vacation home on wheels may not be directly related to rehabbing the camper, but it is essential to preventing disaster. The right trailer hitch efficiently distributes weight and safely secures the camper to the tow vehicle. The wrong hitch makes the camper trailer harder to control during driving, can put excessive wear on the tow-vehicle's drive train, and increases the risk of an accident.

Class I and Class II ball hitches (see table) are known as "weight-carrying" hitches, which simply means the trailer's weight is focused on the ball hitch attachment. These are the least stable hitches, and are subsequently used only to tow light trailers, such as teardrops and small pop-ups. Larger, more complex ball or shank hitches are "weight-distributing," designed to spread the weight along the front and back of the tow vehicle (these are often used with stabilizing systems that limit sway and other problems). Fifth-wheel hitches are the sturdiest and most efficient type, because the towing weight is placed right over the rear axle of the tow vehicle, effectively eliminating any sway and making for a very stable ride.

Determining the correct hitch for your camper and tow vehicle is essential to avoid any weak link that could become a failure point. Be aware, however, that a hitch cannot increase the weight the tow vehicle is capable of pulling. Buying a hitch rated for more weight than your car or truck is rated to pull is a waste of money. You simply want to make sure your tow vehicle is rated to tow the gross vehicle weight (GVW) of the trailer, and that the hitch structure itself is rated that same amount of weight. This is true of any component you change, such as a ball, which must also be rated at or exceeding the GVW.

UNDERSTANDING HITCH CLASSES

Trailer hitches fall into one of four "classes," based on how much weight the hitch can tolerate on the weak point of the tongue (the mating point) and in pulling— known as TW and GVW, respectively. Here are the class designations:

Class	TW	GVW
I	Up to 200 lb.	Up to 2,000 lb.
II	Up to 300 lb.	Up to 3,500 lb.
III	Up to 500 lb.	Up to 5,000 lb.
IV	Up to 1,000 lb.	Up to 10,000 lb.

GVW

When you're figuring out just how large a hitch you'll need for the trailer you've rehabbed, you'll need to consider the gross vehicle weight (GVW) rather than the dry weight from the manufacturer. GVW includes the weight of the trailer with full holding tanks and loaded with supplies.

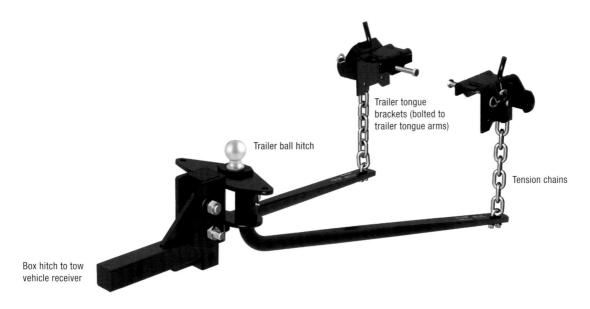

Trailer tongue brackets (bolted to trailer tongue arms)

Trailer ball hitch

Tension chains

Box hitch to tow vehicle receiver

This is a typical weight-distribution ball hitch designed to go into a tow vehicle's box hitch receiver. The system stabilizes the trailer, making it easier and safer to tow. *CURT Manufacturing*

Different hitches will have different parts. It's wise to understand how those parts work to avoid any problems down the road.

- **HITCH BALLS.** The ball size on a ball hitch determines the maximum towing capacity. Hitch balls come in $1\frac{7}{8}$-, 2-, and $2\frac{5}{16}$-inch diameters. The bigger the ball, the more it can tow. The balls are rated from 2,000 to 10,000 pounds. A raised ball with an extender will be rated lower. Make sure the ball is properly installed, with several courses of threads showing below the nut and lock washer. Always use ball grease on a ball when towing.

- **SPRING BARS.** These are used with weight-distributing hitches to equalize weight. They either extend back underneath the trailer or underneath the tow vehicle. Each bar is suspended from a "snap-up" frame bracket that is attached to the frame of the tow vehicle or tow frame under the trailer. The chains are adjusted for the best ride and stability.

- **SAFETY CHAINS.** Safety chains are used on hitches as a fail-safe. Should the hitch connection fail, the trailer will remain attached to the tow vehicle by the chains, preventing a catastrophic runaway trailer.

If you have any doubt about the appropriate hitch, safety features, or sway control system for your tow vehicle and trailer, consult an RV dealer or RV repair shop for advice on which system is best and how to install it—or, better yet, have the pros install and test it.

WINDOWS and DOORS

Camper windows and doors inevitably take a beating. The openings themselves are prone to deform under the stresses and strain of the open road, and bumping into the occasional tree branch or having a door slam open while the trailer is in motion because it hasn't been properly secured can all lead to damage and even complete door or window failure. That's why replacing entry doors, compartment doors, and camper windows are all common older camper rehab issues.

The problem with those replacements is that the openings in campers are not standardized. Any window or door you need to replace may be particular to the manufacturer who created the camper in the first place. The good news is that reproduction manufacturers produce retro parts that are as good as the originals. In the worst-case scenario, you can even have a new window or door fabricated.

HOW TO REPLACE AND RESEAL AN ALUMINUM WINDOW

Rehabbing an older camper inevitably means replacing cracked or deformed windows, or at least resealing them. In either case, doing the job right means pulling the window out of its opening. Take heart, though—that's not a big job. Newer windows are just as handy because all the screws are on the inside half of the frame. You will, however, need a helper when removing a two-piece frame, lest you wind up with a many-piece window.

1   Remove the window by unscrewing the frame from the outside of the camper. If there is a cowl or top piece, unscrew it first. For newer two-piece frames (they will be obvious because no screws will show on the outside), unscrew the frame from the inside and have a helper push it out while you hold and catch it outside.

2   The frame of an older aluminum window will most likely stick in place because of the old sealant. Carefully pry it away from the camper's siding using a thin plastic fid or scraper.

3   Measure the opening carefully. Measure three places along the width and three along the height. If you're ordering a replacement window, use the smallest measurements for the new window dimensions.

4 If you're reusing an existing window, replace any broken or damaged glass. Scrape off any remaining putty or gasket on the inside of the window's flange. Clean around the window opening with rubbing alcohol or mineral spirits and a plastic scraper and a rag.

OPTIONAL: To revive an aluminum frame, tape off and protect the glass with plastic, then spray the frame with aluminum brightener following the instructions on the bottle. Wash off the brightener and polish the frame to the desired sheen with a scrubbing sponge.

5 If you're installing a replacement window, remove it from its packaging and peel off any protective coating. Dry fit the window to ensure the flange overlaps the opening by at least 3/8 inch. Repair any rot in the window frame before proceeding.

6 Line the inside of the window frame flange with butyl tape. Choose a tape width slightly narrower than the flange. Cut a strip for each side to length, press it in place 1/8 to 1/4 inch from the outer edge of the frame, and then remove the protective plastic. Press down the tape at the corners to mate the strips. In the case of a two-piece frame, clean the inside edges of the opening and check that none of the screws is stripped.

7 Stick new stainless-steel screws through the holes in two opposite corners of the frame, poking the screws through the butyl tape. Sit the window in the opening and line the screws up with their holes, sticking them into the holes slightly. Slowly drive the screws into the holes, just so they are almost snug.

8 Drive the screws into the rest of the holes, and make sure they're tightened down without stripping them. Carefully slice off any butyl tape squeeze-out around the edges of the frame using a utility knife or plastic scraper, but be careful not to score the siding. Clean the window and frame with an all-purpose, nonabrasive cleaner.

WHAT YOU'LL NEED

- ☐ Work gloves
- ☐ Eye and ear protection
- ☐ Ladder (optional)
- ☐ Standard screwdriver (optional)
- ☐ Power drill and screwdriver bits
- ☐ Plastic scraper
- ☐ Measuring tape
- ☐ Rubbing alcohol or mineral spirits
- ☐ Rags
- ☐ Painter's tape (optional)
- ☐ Plastic sheeting (optional)
- ☐ Aluminum cleaner-brightener (optional)
- ☐ Scrubbing sponge (optional)
- ☐ New window (optional)
- ☐ Butyl tape
- ☐ Stainless-steel replacement screws
- ☐ Utility knife
- ☐ Window cleaner

HOW TO REPLACE A ROTTED DOOR FRAME

WHAT YOU'LL NEED

- ☐ Work gloves
- ☐ Eye protection
- ☐ Respirator (optional)
- ☐ Power drill and bits
- ☐ Reciprocating saw or jigsaw
- ☐ 2 x 4s
- ☐ Circular saw or table saw
- ☐ Aluminum polish
- ☐ Wire wheel
- ☐ Finish nails
- ☐ Nail gun or hammer
- ☐ Silicone caulk
- ☐ Construction adhesive

Any opening in the wall of a camper is a potential weak spot for water to infiltrate. A door is perhaps the most susceptible opening because the structure is prone to deforming during travel, and an out-of-alignment door exposes the frame to the elements.

That's why rotted door frames are fairly common on older, poorly maintained camper trailers. It's important to address the situation to prevent the rot from spreading into the wall or floor structure.

Repairing a rotted door frame is a challenging project. You have to be exact with your measurements (although you can use existing intact framing members as templates for cutting new members), and you have to be sure to find and remove all the rot.

Keep in mind that before remedying rot in a wall or door structure, you should check the roof and seams for potential leaks. They should be fixed before you repair the rot below.

1 Remove the door by unscrewing the hinges.

2 **TOP LEFT:** Remove the exterior door trim. Set the door and trim aside in a secure area, and save the screws in a resealable plastic bag, to match for new or to ensure you don't misplace them.

3 **TOP RIGHT:** Unscrew and pry away the interior door trim, and remove any rotted sections of interior wall. Here, the rotted door header has infected the wood paneling, and both are being removed.

4 **LEFT:** Pry away the wall surfaces on the inside and outside to gain access to the rotted areas. Assess how far the rot has spread, and use a reciprocating saw to cut out rotted sections. Remove all rotted wood.

5 **TOP LEFT:** Measure the remaining intact framing pieces to determine the correct width for the new framing members. Rip down nominal lumber to the dimensions necessary to reframe the door.

6 **TOP RIGHT:** Screw the new framing members into place to the existing sound members in the wall. Tack the siding to the new framing members with brads.

7 **RIGHT:** Measure and cut a new door header. Coat the bottom of the top plate with construction adhesive and snug the header in place. Screw the header to the top plate and to the jambs on either side.

8 **TOP LEFT:** Where you've had to excise a section of siding to reach rotted wood, lay a bead of silicone caulk along the seams between existing siding and patch. Nail the patch in place (inset).

9 **TOP RIGHT:** Spruce up the door before reinstalling. Use a wire wheel to remove dirt, rust, and grime on aluminum trim and polish the trim with aluminum polish. Adjust the door construction as necessary to square the door.

10 **LEFT:** Measure the diagonals of the door one last time to ensure the opening is square. Lay a bead of caulk along the edge of the siding where it terminates at the door opening. Clean or replace and reinstall the exterior door trim.

HOW TO REPLACE A ROTTED DOOR FRAME (CONTINUED)

11 **TOP LEFT:** Replace the interior trim to match the trim around the windows, or the original door trim. Lay down a bead of silicone caulk before tacking the trim pieces in place.

12 **LEFT AND BELOW:** Hang the door so that it is perfectly aligned within the opening. Check that it opens and closes tightly, then caulk any remaining seams, such as the joints on either side of the threshold.

HOW TO REALIGN A CAMPER DOOR

Inevitably, the long road to your dream campsite is filled with more than its share of bumps and potholes. Because the door to your camper is usually the largest opening in the structure, it's the one most likely to be affected by all the stresses the camper absorbs. Maintaining door alignment is both a safety and an economy issue. You don't want your door flying open at the wrong moment, and a misaligned door will bleed more air-conditioned or heated air from inside the camper.

WHAT YOU'LL NEED

- ☐ Work gloves
- ☐ Eye and ear protection
- ☐ Measuring tape
- ☐ Screwdriver
- ☐ Power drill and bits
- ☐ ⅛"-thick shims
- ☐ Hammer

Keep in mind that the steps that follow describe squaring a door in a standard, aluminum-sided vintage trailer. For newer trailers, or more unique constructions such as Airstream trailers, consult the manufacturer's instructions for door alignment.

1 Remove the interior door molding and inspect all around the opening for obvious defects such as water damage. Measure side to side every few inches down the opening to determine where the doorway is out of square.

2 Remove any frame trim. Begin shimming the door on the hinge side, driving shims between the frame and stud at the points where the door widens out of square.

3 Measure the diagonals from corner to corner to ensure the opening is square. Tighten all the screws holding the frame to the camper wall.

4 Check that the door opens and closes smoothly and securely, and that it locks properly. Replace the trim pieces.

HOW TO REFURBISH EXTERIOR LIGHTING FIXTURES

As part of cleaning or painting the exterior of your new old camper trailer, consider rehabbing all the exterior lighting fixtures. This is your way of inspecting small but important features that are subject to deterioration over exposure to time and the elements.

Not only will refurbishing the exterior lights on the camper serve as a safety check, it's also a way to add sparkle and fresh new look to a cleaned-up trailer. It's a fairly easy chore, requiring a minimum of tools and expertise. You won't need more than a day or two to rehab all the exterior lights on the camper.

1 **BELOW:** Disconnect the battery in the camper and disconnect the camper from any lead vehicle to which the light system is connected. Unscrew the fixture lens. Keep screws that are in good condition, but plan on replacing any rusted fasteners with stainless-steel versions.

2 **RIGHT:** Disconnect the wires to the fixture, unscrew the fixture flange, and remove the backing plate from the camper wall. Remove the bulb and use a wire wheel to clean up both sides of the backing plate and the flange.

WHAT YOU'LL NEED

- ☐ Work gloves
- ☐ Eye and ear protection
- ☐ Screwdriver
- ☐ Stainless-steel screws
- ☐ Power drill and wire wheel
- ☐ Metal spray primer and paint
- ☐ Painter's tape
- ☐ Wire strippers
- ☐ Pliers
- ☐ Wire nuts

3 **TOP RIGHT:** Prime and paint the backing plate, being sure to protect the electrical components with painter's tape.

4 Clean the lens cover. Start with a gentle solution of warm water and dishwashing soap, and use window cleaner if necessary. You may need to soak the lens in a solution of hot water and ammonia to remove stubborn grime and dirt.

5 **MIDDLE RIGHT:** Insert a new bulb into the fixture, and trim and strip the ends of the wires. Do the same for the wires from the camper's electrical system.

6 **BOTTOM RIGHT:** Lay a bead of caulk on the back of the backing plate. Run the wires from the camper through the hole in the backing plate and screw the backing plate in place on the camper. Connect the wires, positive to positive and ground to ground, with wire nuts.

7 Test the light. Once you're sure it's working, install a new gasket in the lens cover and screw it in place over the backing plate using new screws.

AWNINGS

Although many older campers don't have awnings, they're well worth considering as a retrofit. An awning provides shade in campground lots that are frequently located in direct sunlight without any shade. The right awning can create an open-air room right outside the door of the camper, one that allows you to enjoy the benefits of the camper and the beauty of the outdoors at the same time. A window awning can cool the interior a bit, and even provide a measure of privacy.

Whether you're replacing a ripped and worn awning or retrofitting a brand-new one, you should be able to install a manual awning yourself in a single long afternoon with a few basic tools and materials. (An automatic, powered awning requires wiring into the camper's existing system and should usually be handled by a professional installer.)

To start with, get to know the parts of the awning. Basically, an awning will have some sort of extension arms that collapse for travel or when you aren't using the awning; the fabric "drape" that provides the shade; the slide rail (or, in the case of larger or motorized awnings, reinforced brackets) that anchors the roller tube in which the drape is contained when rolled up; the roller tube assembly; and a strap or rod hold-down.

Awning drapes themselves are often made of durable vinyl, treated to resist fading and deterioration from the sun's UV rays. However, custom awning drapes are sometimes crafted of vibrant fabrics treated with protectants and sealers to ensure they resist weather damage. Custom awnings are a way to add a distinctive look to your trailer because most stock awnings are solid neutral colors.

If you need a smaller awning for a distinctive older trailer, it may well be worth the investment to have a custom awning made to match the look of your camper.

3

CAMPER SYSTEMS

You can't have a home away from home without a lot of the same systems that make a house a home. That's why a well-appointed camper trailer includes plumbing, sewage, electrical, and even entertainment systems that echo those in the average house. The good news for any camper DIYer is that many of these systems and their components are simpler than their full-blown residential equivalents. With a little patience and attention to detail, you should be able to maintain, service, troubleshoot, and, yes, even install your camper's systems.

A WIRED HOME ON WHEELS

Perhaps the most important system for making a camper a highly functional living space for even the short term is the electrical system. Electrified campers use a 12-volt direct current (DC) system, a 120-volt alternating current (AC) system, or a combination. Either of these systems can draw power from different sources, including onboard batteries, generators, campground hookups, or even rooftop solar systems, depending on the circumstance.

Regardless of the system, the first item on your checklist should be the over-current protection device (OCPD) that defends against short-circuits and fire. This is usually a master circuit breaker or fuse located close to the power source. If your camper lacks this feature, have one installed.

A simple test light is an inexpensive but valuable addition to your toolbox, one that will help you diagnose electrical problems. (Keep in mind that different types of test probes are used to test for AC and DC power.) If you're willing to spend a little more, buy a multimeter. It allows you to measure a whole lot more in regard to your electrical systems, from checking polarities to measuring circuit resistance and more.

An external port like this one allows campers to "dock," or hook up, to land power lines at campgrounds and when staying on a residential property.

A multimeter is an excellent tool for checking and troubleshooting a camper trailer's electrical system.

Depending on the age, size, and type of camper you own, the structure may have several or all of the features below.

- **GENERATOR.** A generator produces electricity when onboard batteries run out and no shoreline hookup is available. An "inverter" generator can be connected to both a 12-volt and a 120-volt system at the same time, which is why this is the most common RV generator. It allows you to charge your batteries and supply electricity to AC outlets simultaneously. You can choose a gas-, diesel-, or propane-powered generator. Even if your camper doesn't have an onboard generator, it's easy to connect a standalone aftermarket unit.

- **BATTERIES.** Camper electrical systems typically use two types of batteries—the tow vehicle's cranking battery that's appropriate for short bursts as needed and deep-cycle batteries that deliver low-amp current for camper fixtures and some appliances (you can identify DC-powered appliances by the "lighter plug" cord end). There are, in turn, three types of deep-cycle batteries: wet cell (or "flooded electrolyte"), gel, and absorbed glass mat (AGM). All three come in 6-volt and 12-volt capacities. Wet cell batteries are the most common, delivering excellent charge capacity at a low cost.

Using campground shoreline hookups can reduce the need for a large battery array or a generator but can limit where you camp.

The downside to wet cell batteries is that they require maintenance because the electrolytic action inside the battery evaporates the water in the cell, which needs to be refilled periodically to avoid damaging or destroying the battery. Gel and AGM require no maintenance but are appreciably more expensive for roughly the same charging capacity. All deep-cycle batteries are

THE DEEP CYCLE RULES

Deep-cycle RV batteries aren't cheap, so the goal is to make them last as long as possible by avoiding sulfation, a condition in which lead sulfate compounds form on the battery's plates. Sulfation interferes with battery function and can lead to early battery death.

1 Discharge correctly. Experts recommend keeping any depth of discharge above 50 percent of battery charge.

2 Don't mix. When you have to replace a deep-cycle battery, replace its companions at the same time, to prevent destructive charging patterns. You can, however, replace a failed battery with a used one of the same size, age, and usage history.

3 Hydrate carefully. Deep-cycle battery "gassing" is a natural part of the discharge-recharge cycle, and causes evaporation of the water in flooded deep-cycle batteries (the most common type). You'll need to periodically add water. Use only distilled water and fill the cells to about $1/8$ inch below the top of the vent well, and never let it drop below the top of the battery's plates. Add water only after the battery is charged.

4 Don't overcharge. Continuous charging can damage or destroy the plates.

5 Check the cables. Corroded cables can be the source of many different problems in a 12-volt system. Make sure the terminals and exposed portions of the cable are corrosion free. Clean cables and terminals, once disconnected, with a solution of baking soda and water. Shorter and thicker cables (8-gauge cable is usually used for this reason) bleed less electricity in transmission.

designed to be continuously depleted (although not fully—the percentage of charge lost is called the "depth of discharge") and recharged.

Battery life spans are radically affected by how much you use the camper, exposure to temperature extremes, and other variables. Testing your deep-cycle batteries on a regular basis is a good idea. There are a number of ways to do this, but the most common and simplest is to use a hydrometer, available at RV and automotive supply stores. RV repair shops will test batteries to see how well they hold a charge and how quickly they lose charge under load.

Power-hogging gadgets, such as big-screen TVs, washers and dryers, and faux fireplace heating units, aren't too big a problem if you plan on plugging in at a campsite, but if you're going off the grid, you'll need to make sure you have enough juice.

As you rehab your camper, you may choose to add some power-sucking conveniences, from microwave ovens to washing machines. That's not a battery issue if you plan on staying almost exclusively at campsites or locations where there is a connection for your shoreline. However, if you are planning on boondocking—camping entirely off the grid—then your battery bank is going to be a key source of power right along with a generator. The trick is figuring out just how many batteries you need in that bank.

There are several ways to calculate battery capacity requirements, but all are relative. For instance, if you're a "roughing it" camper who reads at night by the light of a kerosene lamp and you don't care for appliances in your outdoor experiences, your power needs will be modest. If you crave a little more comfort and convenience, you could be looking at clocking a lot of amp hours.

Calculate the battery capacity you'll require by noting the power consumption ratings on appliance and fixture labels. Start with the continuous power rating for something like a coffeemaker (typically about 1400 watts). Plug that number into this formula:

$$\frac{\text{AC watts}}{12} \times 1.1 \times \text{hours of operation} = \text{battery DC amp hours}$$

For DC-powered appliances (i.e., incandescent light—1.2 amps—or a TV—6 amps continuous), multiply the number by the hours of use to get the total battery amp hours. Make these calculations for all the appliances you'll regularly use in a day. Total up the battery amp hours, and then double it (remember, you don't want to discharge batteries below 50 percent). That's the minimum battery capacity you need from the total number of deep-cycle batteries in your bank.

INVERTER AND CONVERTER

Unless it's been upgraded, your older camper trailer is probably outfitted with a converter rather than an inverter. A converter simply converts AC power from a shoreline or other outside connection (such as an external generator) into DC power for the camper's DC-powered appliances and fixtures, such as interior lights, entertainment system, and water pump. Converters also slowly charge deep-cycle batteries. Older and less expensive units are relatively inefficient and often make an annoying buzzing sound. They can cause power spikes that damage appliances, and they take a long time to charge batteries. When you're running off-grid on battery power alone, the converter won't produce AC power, meaning you can't charge your phone, run a blender, or dry your hair.

An inverter, on the other hand, turns DC power into usable AC, allowing you to use AC-powered appliances and fixtures when there is no shoreline connection and you don't want to or can't run a generator. Inverters do have limitations, however. They pull a lot of juice from the batteries, so it's wise to limit AC appliance use to one at a time when your're on battery power running through the inverter. The best type of inverter for camper use is a "pure sine wave" unit; the other type, "modified sine wave," can potentially play havoc with certain appliances and equipment. You can also buy combination converter-inverters that do both functions. They're more expensive, but they are also more versatile.

Camper wiring systems can take a lot of abuse due to temperature extremes, bumpy roads, and potential exposure to moisture. Check your wiring regularly and keep it in good repair.

WIRING

Sounds pretty basic, right? Wiring—what could go wrong?

Well, a lot, as it turns out, because the wiring in a used camper has possibly been exposed to temperature extremes and movement that can cause chafing and wear. Wiring that was once affixed to the frame may have come loose. Regularly check your wiring, especially any that passes through walls; the wires should still be protected from sharp hole edges by grommets. For the same reason, check for any relatively loose wires that might move during transit and rub against metal parts. Play it safe and cover those runs with plastic conduit. A short in a line is a simple problem, but it can be amazingly difficult to find and fix if the run of wire travels throughout the camper's structure.

GFCI OUTLETS

All new camper trailers are equipped with ground fault circuit interrupter (GFCI) outlets anywhere water is a factor, such as bathrooms and kitchens. The outlets are designed to protect against shock and shorts that could cause fire. GFCIs are also used to protect external outlets. However, if you've got your hands on a vintage beauty, she may have no GFCIs whatsoever. Play it smart and replace the outlets in the bath area and in the kitchen with GFCI outlets. Then test the GFCIs before every camping trip.

THE SOLAR CAMPER

Once considered an esoteric add-on, solar power systems are a common upgrade to campers these days. The technology has come a long way from the early days. Not only are photovoltaic (PV) cells that make up modern panels much more efficient at converting the sun's rays into electricity, but also the panels themselves are now available in the traditional rigid format or newer roll-out, super-thin, self-adhesive flexible panels. Either option is lightweight and durable—although rigid panels can be fit with adjustable legs, so that they can be angled toward the sun, making them more efficient.

There are many turnkey RV solar kits available, but you can also buy the components separately if you like the idea of designing a system customized for your rig. (You can also get your feet wet with a portable solar panel that can be attached to your batteries to recharge them during the day.) A 200-watt, all-in-one quality solar kit can be had for less than $1,000, and could provide all the daytime power and battery charging capability you would need for a camping trip with appliances and no shoreline hookup.

In any case, buy monocrystalline PV panels rather than polycrystalline or solar film. (Monocrystalline cells are far more efficient.) The majority of systems for sale include two panels that are wired in series. It's easy to add panels later—available roof space notwithstanding—if you find your energy needs are greater than you anticipated.

Next to the panels and cells, the charge controller is the most important part of the system. The controller regulates the charge going to the battery and, without it, the panels could drain the batteries when the sun goes down and the PV cells no longer produce electricity. There are two types of controller: PWM (pulse width modulation) and MPPT (maximum power point tracking). MPPT controllers are superior and worth spending more to upgrade if your kit comes with a PWM controller.

RIGHT: If you're not ready to commit to roof-mounted panels on your camper, portable panel systems are a great way to try the technology out.

SAFETY FIRST!

It's important to keep in mind any time you're working with solar panels that, unless they are covered with an opaque material, they are capable of producing electricity. Always treat any uncovered solar panel as a live electrical fixture.

HOW TO INSTALL AN RV SOLAR SYSTEM

You don't need to be an electrician to install a solar system in your camper, but you will need a basic understanding of how electrical circuits work. Expect to spend a weekend (choose one with no rain in the forecast) installing and checking the system. If you doubt your electrical or DIY abilities, it may be well worth your money to spend a couple hundred dollars having the local RV service center install and test the system.

1. Determine the location for the panels on the roof of the camper. Select an area that will not be shaded by nearby structures, such as an air-conditioning unit hood, and that will be close to where you want to route the system cables (cables are often routed down a waste tank vent). Measure and mark the exact location.

2. Unbox all the components and check that you have all the hardware you'll need. Clean the installation area thoroughly. If you're using flexible panels, the surface has to be absolutely free of dirt, grease, or foreign substances that might prevent the panels from adhering securely to the roof.

3. Check the voltage on the panels with a multimeter to ensure they are not damaged. Leave the panels covered if possible, to block the sun and stop the panels from producing current.

   NOTE: *You can also work indoors, such as in a garage, to prevent the panels from producing significant current.*

4. Attach the Z brackets to the panels (or to the sliding guides for adjustable panels). Mark the holes for the Z bracket feet on the roof of the camper and drill pilot holes for the bracket screws.

5. Lay a dab of sealant caulk in the screw holes before attaching the feet to the roof. Cover the Z bracket feet and the screw or bolt head with a liberal bead of sealant caulk once the panel is fastened down.

   NOTE: *Select the appropriate tape and sealant for the roof you have—rubber will require different sealant than fiberglass or aluminum. You can also provide additional protection against leaks by laying down a square of sealant tape under each Z bracket foot.*

ALTERNATIVE: If you're using flexible panels, peel back the plastic covering the adhesive from one edge. Line up the edge with the marks on the roof and, as you continue peeling the plastic, press the rest of the panel down into position. Completely smooth it out all over the surface, being careful to press out all air bubbles.

WHAT YOU'LL NEED

- ☐ Work gloves
- ☐ Eye and ear protection
- ☐ Ladder
- ☐ Measuring tape
- ☐ Carpenter's pencil or grease pencil
- ☐ Solar panel(s)
- ☐ Solar panel mounting kit
- ☐ Cleaner
- ☐ Multimeter
- ☐ Power drill and bits
- ☐ Lap sealant (sealant caulk, matched to the roof material)
- ☐ Sealant tape (matched to the roof material)
- ☐ Cable or wire clamps
- ☐ Socket wrench and sockets
- ☐ Wire cutters

6 Plan the best path for the power cables down to the battery compartment. (A waste tank vent is a great option because any leaks drain into the gray water tank.) Drill a hole for the cables alongside the vent pipe or down into a refrigerator vent. Mark each end of what will be the positive cable with tape, and feed the cables down into the hole. Route the cables as needed, using ties and wire clamps to secure the cables along their route.

7 Attach the controller to the wall of the battery compartment with the supplied screws. Connect the power cables from the panel to the inputs on the controller, and connect the battery cables from the controller to the batteries, following the manufacturer's hookup instructions—cutting and splicing wires as necessary.

OPTION: Your system may have come with a meter controller with a readout, meant to be mounted inside the camper. If so, run the cable from the controller up to the closest convenient location from the battery compartment, and cut an access hole in the mounting location (usually a false cabinet front or similar area).

8 Return to the roof and hook up the panels to the power cables. Follow the manufacturer's directions for connecting multiple panels (they are usually connected in series). Remove any covering over the panels. Check the readout on the solar controller to ensure that current is flowing from the panels into the batteries.

9 Secure the rooftop cables with sealant tape. Check that all the cable entry points through the roof are protected with lap sealant and that the mounting bracket feet are also securely covered with sealant. If you installed flexible panels, lay a bead of sealant around the perimeter of each panel to ensure that water and wind don't infiltrate underneath the panel.

HEAVY DUTY

Whenever you have the option, use heavier gauge wire in a solar system. Heavier gauge wires reduce line loss of electricity, especially over long runs of wire.

COMMUNICATION AND ENTERTAINMENT SYSTEMS

Camping has become increasingly sophisticated as new advances in trailer retrofit technology hit the market, outdoor adventurers hit the road for longer and longer vacations (or even lifestyle changes), and the idea of "staying connected" has become universal. The fact of the matter is that today's campers—and especially glampers—want the flexibility of watching a movie after a long day of hiking, touching base with friends or family, and checking email as the need or desire arises. New technology allows for all that and more. But as with many things in rehabbing a camper, when it comes to mobile connectivity, the tradeoff is always efficiency versus cost. Let's start with the internet.

A standalone satellite dish is often easier to arrange for signal reception than a roof-mounted model, but it does take up a lot of storage space on board a camper trailer.

ROAD-GOING INTERNET

Having access to a stable internet connection is about more than just checking your email on a regular basis. More and more campers are choosing to take longer working getaways, because they can be just as productive in the comfortable confines of their rehabbed camper. The internet can also be an entertainment solution for campers looking to stream movies or TV shows through services such as Netflix or Hulu. The trick is to maintain a strong, fast connection no matter where you are. There are basically three technologies to help you do that: cellular, Wi-Fi, and satellite.

The longer you're away, the more likely you are to want internet access at some point on your camper excursion.

CELLULAR

Your smart phone may be all you need for modest email and internet use. Some phones can even be used as a mobile Wi-Fi hotspot (check your "settings" options) that can serve as a Wi-Fi beacon for other electronics. However, you'll face that persistent problem of cell tower reception. The signal may be blocked by any number of obstructions that stop your phone from picking up or maintaining a decent reliable signal.

Cellular antennas can help, and boosters can strengthen the signal inside your camper. You can even use an antenna in conjunction with a device known as a jetpack, which grabs an incoming cellular signal and creates a Wi-Fi hotspot that doesn't move with your phone. You can also turn to a router with a cellular antenna built in. It's another way to improve signal strength and reach.

All these options are naturally going to be limited by the data plan you're on, while available reception will be reliant on the coverage of your provider. That's why cellular internet is best for light usage and as a backup option.

WI-FI

This can be an extremely handy option for campers who want to access the internet on a regular basis, don't want spend a ton of money, and usually camp at established RV parks. However, there are limitations. Think of the Wi-Fi service as a pipe. The pipe doesn't get bigger the more users there are, or if users are streaming bandwidth-hogging content like high-definition movies.

The same size "pipe" services the RV park whether there are 10 campers or 100. The truth is, Wi-Fi is simply not super efficient. And if you think you'll regularly pick up a signal by swinging by a Starbucks or other retail establishment that offers free Wi-Fi, you may want to rethink that plan. Whereas RV parks have equipment that is intended to broadcast the Wi-Fi signal across the park, stores tend to use equipment meant to localize the signal precisely because they don't want walk-by (or parked) outsiders strangling the bandwidth.

You can, however, boost the signals at a park or in front of a friend's house with a line-of-sight antenna—or if you are willing to part with a hefty bit of your hard-earned cash, you can buy a roof-mounted omnidirectional antenna that lays flat for travel and flips up when you need it. All in all, Wi-Fi can be a good option for camping internet access, but it is dependent on where you're staying and how many other people are using the signal.

SATELLITE

This is the most expensive option but potentially the most efficient and powerful for the camper who wants to work full or part time on the road. If you can grab an unimpeded satellite signal, you'll enjoy fast, reliable internet service. The key word there is "if." To access satellite signals, you need a clear view of the southern sky, because most satellites circle the Earth roughly along the equator. That means that if you're nestled in the forest among scenic towering old-growth trees, you're not going to get a satellite signal. (But, then again, you're probably not going to get a Wi-Fi or cell signal either. As long as you do have a clear shot at the signal, you'll often be able to access it when there's no cell tower or Wi-Fi network in range.)

The expensive part of satellite internet is the antenna. The best antennas are dishes, and they come as portable standalones mounted on a tripod or as roof-mounted dishes. They'll run from around $1,000 to more than $5,000. You can opt for the less-expensive "dome" versions, but they are also less effective and more prone to rain and snow interference.

CALLING ALL CAMPERS

Phones are not just a camping convenience; they can be crucial when you need roadside assistance for your tow vehicle or in the event you use your phone as your GPS. The key to staying connected is signal strength. That becomes a challenge when you're out of range of a cell tower or surrounded by natural barriers to a cell tower signal. The problem is compounded by the fact that many camper trailers are in and of themselves metal, signal-blocking boxes. The answer is to employ a signal booster. The principle behind boosters is simple: the signal is picked up by an antenna (mounted on the roof in the window of the camper) and then routed through an amplifier that strengthens it in close proximity to the phone. There are two basic types that campers can choose from: mobile and fixed.

- **MOBILE.** Mobile boosters are designed to pick up signals whether the camper is in motion or parked. These are often used by motorhome owners who want to get a good signal while driving. Because camper trailer or truck camper owners are usually only inside the structure when it's parked, a fixed booster makes more sense.

- **FIXED.** These are the stronger option and come with one of two types of antenna: omni or directional. Omni antennas are automatic and are designed to pick up signals from any direction. Consequently, they require no setup. Directional antennas are better at picking up distance signals, but they need to be adjusted to the optimal angle and direction.

TV ON THE GO

If you're only interested in occasionally streaming a movie or TV show, it's quite possible you can get by using your cellular service or local Wi-Fi when it's available. This option works only if you're willing to forego entertainment options when you can't pick up a signal. Otherwise, you'll be using a satellite dish.

TVs like this are commonly included in both newer trailers and rehabbed older campers. But the hardware is only as good as the service you get in your location.

Let's be clear here. Even though providers advertise satellite combination packages for TV and internet, the two streams are vastly different animals. A TV signal travels one way and it's a known quantity—especially a streamed file of an existing movie. It gets beamed to the satellite and the satellite beams it to your dish. Easy peasy, and not particularly challenging for the technology to handle. internet, on the other hand, is a two-way signal. You receive a signal providing you with your email, and then you reply with a signal sending an email. Downloading a file puts a variable burden on the system, and loading different websites may require different data transfer specifics. That's a much more complicated data stream. That difference is why combo packages work much better in the static location of a home, rather than the moving target of a camper. Here again, your reception relies on the quality of your satellite dish, which at any level can be pricey.

RADIO IN THE WILDS

Maybe you're looking for a dose of NPR while you enjoy the scenery in your favorite campgrounds, want the easy alternative of turning on your favorite rock oldies station, or can't live without the latest on your favorite sports team. AM or FM radio through standard broadcast is going to be hard to find in most far-flung camping locales—the signals are simply not strong enough to travel the distance necessary. A satellite beam, though, is often up to the challenge. No wonder, then, that campers and RVers often choose satellite radio services to get their favorite stations both while traveling and while camping out. The service will require a satellite-equipped radio and a high-quality satellite antenna. Fortunately, these are much less expensive than their satellite TV cousins—a good satellite radio antenna will run you less than $100.

STEREO SYSTEMS

As beautiful as the sounds of nature can be, sometimes it's nice to bring your own playlist along on your camping adventures. That means having something to play the tunes (or podcasts) on. Thank goodness there is a wealth of options.

You'll find an astounding array of aftermarket radios, CD players, and speakers designed specifically for use in RVs and campers. These are wired directly into the DC or AC systems (depending on what type of stereo you buy) and are usually installed by an installer at the time of purchase—although replacing an older stereo is a doable DIY task that involves using the existing wiring.

These days, though, wired-in stereo systems are giving way to portable options that offer comparable acoustics and a lot more flexibility. You'll find music player docks from the low end to ultra expensive, including models that include the ability to receive AM/FM and satellite radio, hook up directly to music players, and play CDS. You can supplement portable stereo systems with sophisticated rechargeable Bluetooth speakers, which allow you to fully customize your system and your camping music experience.

CAMPER ENTERTAINMENT HARDWARE

These days, a great many campers expect to at least be able to watch a DVD movie on their camping trips. Others want to be able to stream entertainment content, and those who spend long periods in their campers may prefer a full-blown satellite TV package. But no matter what you use it for, you'll want a TV that can survive your trips intact and give you a picture you enjoy.

That translates to a TV meant specifically for RV use. Typical home TVs are likely to malfunction under the shaking and physical abuse of traveling in a camper. There's also the issue of power. Whereas home TVs are universally AC powered, RV TVs are often DC powered, or they offer the flexibility of using different power sources in different situations. You can find models that include built-in DVD players and the same options as in home TVs. But RV models are built to withstand shaking and other damaging forces. Likewise, manufacturers produce CD and DVD players to RV standards, as travel equipment. Lastly, invest in a quality TV mount meant for use in campers and RVs, to ensure that your hardware will be securely held in place at all times.

CAMPER PLUMBING

The basic plumbing system used by just about every water-equipped camper on the road is surprisingly simple. But the devil is in the details. Each component plays a part and has its own requirements.

- **FRESHWATER TANK.** The freshwater (or "potable water") tank is one of two sources for clean, fresh drinking, bathing, and faucet water in the camper (the other is the city water hookup, below). The challenge with this part of the plumbing picture is keeping the "fresh" in freshwater. The tank should be rinsed and sanitized after every trip and for winterizing. Only use a certified "potable water" hose to fill your freshwater tank, because the hose is specially designed to impart no odors or taste to the water.

- **CITY WATER HOOKUP.** Yes, it's just a simple hookup, but actually, it's not so simple. There are two dangers with city water sources: dirt and debris in the line, and pressure. Nobody wants to drink—or bathe in—dirty water. Which is why it's a good idea to retrofit your system with an in-line water filter downstream of the city water connection (these aren't a standard feature on campers). Excess plumbing pressure in the lines can cause all kinds damage; the solution is a regulator.

HOSE HEALTH

Keep your fresh potable water hose separate from any other hoses—specifically from the gray and black water hoses. Use them only for the freshwater tank and city water hookup. And sanitize freshwater hoses every time you sanitize the freshwater tank.

Before heading off this problem, it helps to know the difference between *flow* and *pressure*. Flow is the amount of water that comes through the line in a given amount of time, and variable flow rates don't really hurt your plumbing (although low-flow in the shower can make for a disappointing morning ritual). Pressure, on the other hand, is a measure of the force of the water—force that is exerted against the walls of pipes and hoses and can compromise

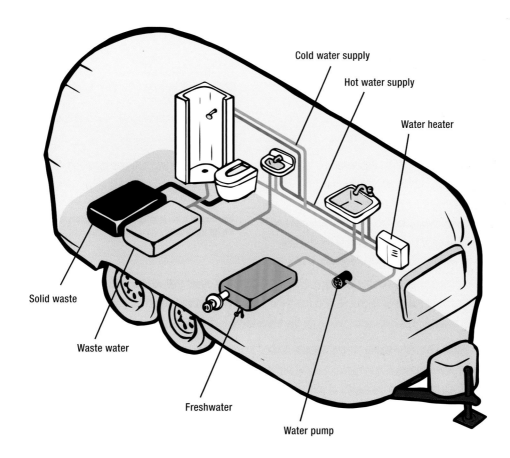

Cold water supply

Hot water supply

Water heater

Solid waste

Waste water

Freshwater

Water pump

the structure, causing them to burst. Think of it as the difference between your pulse rate and your blood pressure.

Regulators are installed between the city source end of the hose and the camper's water source. Although all regulators effectively limit water pressure, and consequently ensure the longevity of your plumbing lines and fixtures, some severely limit flow as well. More expensive regulators are designed to avoid flow problems.

- **FIXTURES.** Keep your toilet, faucets, and other fixtures in good working order to prevent any problems. Twice a year, inspect faucet aerators for debris. Clean or replace any with evidence of buildup. If your showerhead is spraying an irregular pattern, soak it in a 1:1 solution of vinegar and water for an hour.

- **GRAY AND BLACK WATER TANKS.** The downside to having a toilet and plumbing that you can take with you is that you have to bring a sewer as well. The black water tank is dedicated to the toilet, and the gray water to all other drains. Both must be regularly drained down approved waste drains—either at RV parks or at home. The importance of keeping these tanks clean can't be overstated. If they get too dirty, not only will the tank monitors be more likely to misread the tank levels, but

You can fit a surprising amount of luxury into a camper trailer bathroom.

you're also risking clogs within the plumbing system and very bad odors that will be hard to eliminate. So regular emptying of the tanks is crucial, and using the correct process and equipment are key to making it as bearable as possible. The hose and hookup for the black water tank should have a special odorless fitting.

- **WATER PUMP.** The water pump in your camper is used to move water out of the freshwater tank only, because city water comes into the system under pressure. Most camper water pumps are reliable, long-lasting fixtures, but you can ensure the health of your water pump by properly winterizing the water system and following correct fill and emptying procedures for the freshwater tank. (You'll find troubleshooting strategies for common water pump issues on page 180.)

- **WATER HEATER.** Hot water is a one of the nicest luxuries in a camper. There are few things as rejuvenating as a long, soothing shower after a day spent in the woods, or as convenient as washing dinner dishes in sudsy hot water. But a reliable hot water supply means taking care of your onboard water heater. Regular maintenance ensures the unit uses the least amount of energy and guarantees the longest life possible from this expensive appliance.

  The number-one maintenance practice is replacing the anode rod at least once a year. This is a simple habit that most affects water longevity because the anode rod is a sacrificial element that draws corrosion away from the metal body of the water heater. (Aluminum water heaters don't need an anode rod.) The anode rod should be replaced anytime there is less than half the original thickness remaining. Play it safe by replacing an anode rod with one of the same material—magnesium for magnesium, zinc for zinc.

  Beyond the anode rod, a periodic flushing and deep cleaning removes limescale, debris, and other buildup that can interfere with the efficient functioning of the water heater, and can pollute the water that comes out of the hot water side of your faucets. That debris can clog water lines and showerheads, and can deteriorate any fixture.

Here are guidelines for making a nasty job less nasty and keeping your onboard sewer system problem free:

- Regularly use a holding tank deodorizer and waste digester.

- Do not let your waste tanks become completely full before dumping.

- Do not leave the black tank valve open when connected to an RV dump site. You want fluids to accumulate to help move the solids out of the tank when you drain it.

- Dump the black tank first, then the gray tank, which will clean the dump hose of any solids.

- Do not rely on tank monitors to be accurate. Develop a sense of usage patterns as they relate to tank levels, because monitors often become blocked and misread tank levels.

- Add 1 to 2 gallons of water with cleaning enzyme to the black tank after you've dumped, right before leaving a campsite. The action of the water and cleanser sloshing around on the trip home will help scrub the sides of the tank, removing stuck solids. Empty the tank before permanently parking the camper.

- Clean the tank after dumping, using a wash sprayer—a wand that is stuck down through the toilet into the tank, and creates a forceful 360-degree spray. (These may not work with some larger fifth wheels in which the black tank is located further from the toilet.)

HOW TO CHANGE THE ANODE ROD

When working around a water heater, always wear safety glasses and thick rubber work gloves. This same process can be used to flush and clean a water heater that doesn't have an anode rod.

1. Turn off all sources of power to the water heater and check that the water heater is off. Let it cool overnight.

2. Remove the water tank closet cover. Open the pressure-relief "pop up" valve.

3. Remove the drain plug/anode. Be prepared for a rush of water.

4. Fit a tank-rinsing wand onto the end of a garden hose, turn the hose on high, and rinse out the interior until the water runs clear.

5. Wrap the threads of a new anode rod in Teflon tape and install the rod as tight as possible with a socket wrench (don't overtighten).

6. Use a can of compressed air fitted with a nozzle straw to blow any debris out of the burner feed tube and the burner cavity.

7. Close the pressure-relief valve, refill the hot water heater, and turn the power back on/ignite the burner. Open the hot water side of all faucets and let it run until clear. Check the faucet aerators for debris and clean or replace them as necessary.

HOW TO DEEP CLEAN A CAMPER WATER HEATER

This process involves using the power of vinegar's acetic acid to clean limescale and buildup out of the bottom of the tank and off the heating element. It will involve heating the tank of fluid and then emptying it. Use extreme caution when following these instructions to avoid burns.

1   Turn off the power and drain the water heater as you would for replacing the anode rod. Replace the anode rod with a drain plug.

2   Fill the water heater with a mixture of vinegar and water (or pure vinegar for faster results) as far you can by removing the pressure-relief valve and pouring the mixture in through a flexible funnel.

3   Replace the pressure-relief valve and fill the water heater the rest of the way with water from a city source.

4   Close the bypass valves to isolate the water heater from the rest of the plumbing. Turn on the gas and power so that the water heater heats the mixture. Leave it for 5 to 12 hours.

5   Turn off the power and gas to the water heater and let it cool down for several hours. Open the pressure-relief valve and remove the drain plug, being careful to avoid the stream.

6   Use a rinse wand on a garden hose to thoroughly rinse out the tank. Replace the anode rod and close the pressure relief valve.

TOILET TIPS

Nobody wants to deal with black-tank problems. Fortunately, there are a number of strategies that will help keep your camper waste system in good working order and limit your contact and interaction with the dreaded black tank.

- Use toilet paper specially designated for use in RV chemical toilets. This breaks down more quickly and more thoroughly than standard toilet paper does.

- Fill the toilet bowl with water before flushing whenever you have solids or paper in the bowl.

- If your tank sensor does not read empty after you dump the black tank, try emptying a 5-gallon bucket full of warm water down the toilet. Let the water sit for 15 to 20 minutes, then empty the tank again.

HEATING AND COOLING

Whether it's fiberglass or aluminum, your camper is essentially a box on wheels. Most are not well insulated, making them susceptible to variations in temperature. Proper heating and air-conditioning not only make the interior space more comfortable at all times, but they can also make the camper usable in colder months.

It doesn't have to be the middle of winter for temps to fall into the teeth-chattering range. Try camping at altitude in the mountains and the chill after the sun goes down can make you wonder whether it really is early summer. Same goes for the desert at night.

FURNACE

If you have a larger or newer camper trailer, you may have an onboard, ducted, forced-air furnace. These are usually propane powered and, because they've been built for your unit, are efficient at heating the space quickly, as well as precisely adjustable. Depending on the age of your furnace, it may have a basic manual ignition system that needs to be lit with a match—called a standing pilot. This type of pilot light remains on, even when the furnace is off, unless it is accidentally blown out. Electric spark igniters are ignited with an electric circuit controlled by a button. The most advanced units use a completely electronic ignition.

Onboard furnaces have a number of redundant safety features that ensure against overheating or gas leakage. The problem with them is energy use. They use both propane and electricity to power a blower. To avoid the issue of oxygen consumption, they exhaust warm air and pull in cold from the outside before warming it and blowing it into the space. These are also complex systems in a camper, and servicing and repair are best left to professionals. Even with the help of professionals, though, older camper trailers are rarely retrofitted with an onboard furnace because of the space and ductwork needed for the system.

CATALYTIC INFRARED HEATER

These ventless propane devices heat people and things, not air. That makes them very efficient at heating the small confines of a camper (as bodies and objects become hot, they produce heat that, in turn, heats the air). The downside to this technology is that it consumes oxygen. Use a catalytic converter and you'll need an inch of open window for every 1,000 BTUs the heater is rated. Most do have an oxygen depletion sensor, a safety feature that shuts down the heater when the surrounding oxygen level falls below a preset norm. Some can be connected to your propane system, while smaller portable units use disposable gallon propane canisters. They burn a lot of

PROPANE RAIN

Be aware that any propane heater creates significant condensation as a side effect of operation. Using one consistently without proper ventilation, including during the day in cold weather, will lead to moisture problems, such as countertop delamination and even mold.

CHOOSING A HEATER SIZE

The best way to save energy and ensure your own comfort is to choose a heater with a BTU output that matches the size of the area you need to heat. Keep in mind that heating a camper often involves some compromises. For instance, if you only use the bedroom to slide under a big comfy down comforter, you might want to shut the bedroom off when heating the camper, until it's time for bed.

< 200 sq. ft. = 6,000 BTU
< 300 sq. ft. = 10,000 BTU
< 700 sq. ft. = 20,000 BTU
< 1,000 sq. ft. = 30,000 BTU

fuel quickly, so be prepared to go through propane at a fast clip regardless of what the source is. Catalytic heaters are also low maintenance, requiring no more than an occasional dusting and replacement of the catalyst pad every three years.

A variation on the catalytic heater, the *ceramic infrared heater* uses a set of ceramic "bricks" as heat dispersers. They otherwise run in much the same manner as the catalytic heaters, except that the bricks can get glowing hot, so you have to be careful not to place any flammable materials near the front, and to stay far away to avoid burns.

BLUE-FLAME HEATERS

These are the latest in portable heater technology. They work on the convection principle, pulling cool air in at the bottom of the unit and heating it so that it naturally rises out of the top of the heater. It creates more of a dispersed than a focused heat, but it's also safer to use than a brick or even a catalytic heater. The front doesn't get hot enough to burn skin or ignite flammable material. The more expensive versions of this heater are built to resemble fireplaces. The look can be nice for a camper, but it can also be a challenge to leave enough room around the heater for proper airflow.

ELECTRIC SPACE HEATERS

There are a lot of pluses to recommend an electric heater. You can pick one that is just right for the size of your camper trailer, and it is entirely controllable—you set the heat to the temperature you want. You also don't have to worry about the combustion, condensation, and oxygen-consuming issues you would with a catalytic heater. Electric heaters are also relatively expensive. They can be a wonderful aftermarket option for anyone who normally camps at a well-equipped park with an electrical hookup. However, if you're fond of boondocking, electric heaters are not going to serve you as well. They are energy hogs and can run down a battery pack in less than a night.

CHILL OUT

For most outdoor adventurer types, prime camping season means the warmest months of the year. But warm can also mean scorching hot, especially when the only space available is unshaded and blistered with direct sun. At times like that, a camper of any sort can seem less like comfy living quarters and more like an Easy-Bake Oven.

Enter one of the great luxuries of modern camping—air conditioning. The ability to cool off the inside of a camper can make or a break a camping trip, especially one that takes you to the heart of a desert or along a sunny, treeless coastline. A fan can certainly move air around and provide a small measure of relief, but nothing can substitute for the chill of true AC on a 90-degree day.

If you've chosen a modern-era camper as your rehab project, a roof-mounted air conditioner may be part of the package. As complicated as they are, RV air conditioners are also reliable and durable: they're made to withstand the vibration and jolting of a road trip. As long as there's no obvious damage to the unit and it's functional, there's not much you need to do to maintain the AC (the chemical refrigerant doesn't naturally dissipate, and the air conditioner won't normally need to be recharged unless there's been a leak).

An evaporative cooler uses less power and demands less maintenance than air conditioning, but it's not the best option for humid or extremely hot conditions.

If you own an older camper, especially a more modest model, then there's a good chance it came without air conditioning. Never fear: you have options. Older campers can be retrofitted with either a plain window unit or the more expensive option of a true RV unit permanently installed in the roof (that basically just involves cutting a hole in the roof). Either way, it's wise to keep in mind that air-conditioning units are some of the biggest energy hogs a camper can have. If you're retrofitting one, plan on beefing up your energy systems to match.

Regardless of the type of air conditioner you're using in your camper, keeping it clean is the first step in heading off problems and ensuring the unit operates as efficiently as possible. At the start of each season, remove the shroud from a roof-mounted unit and clean the interior of the unit (a can of compressed air is the best way to do this). If you're using a window unit, remove the outer metal shell and blow compressed air over the condenser lines. For either type, clean or replace the air filter pads (it's wise to do this for every trip during the season).

SAFETY FIRST

Any problem involving an air conditioner's refrigerant is a problem for a certified technician. The chemical refrigerant used in air conditioners is under pressure and dangerous in its own right; it's not a DIY issue.

An evaporative cooler (also called a swamp cooler) is an alternative to an air conditioner. Although it won't cool as completely as an AC unit—and doesn't work as well in humid climates—it uses far less energy and is a simpler, low-maintenance appliance. The science behind this device is simple: hot air is passed through a water-soaked mat and cools as the water evaporates. There are very few manufacturers of swamp coolers for campers, simply because of the limitations of the device. But it can be an alternative for campers who find themselves boondocking frequently.

TIPS FOR BACKING UP A TRAVEL TRAILER

One of the most difficult how-tos for any camper trailer owner to master is also one of the most basic: backing the trailer into a campsite spot. Unfortunately, it's a skill that you can't offload to a technician or RV shop. But fear not: all it takes is a little patience and some simple guidelines and you'll be a back-up master in no time flat. Here are the rules.

- **Make the most of your mirrors.** Before you start, adjust the side mirrors to give you the best possible view of what you're doing. You'll find it can help to angle the mirrors slightly down, so that you can see the wheels of the trailer.

- **Check the landing spot.** Having a good visual sense where curbs, tree limbs, potholes, and other potential obstructions lie is key to avoiding damage when backing up a travel trailer. You also need to make sure you know where people, pets, and children are—especially those that don't belong to you.

- **Drive past the site.** The best place to start your approach is a car or truck length past the site.

- **Think "crank in the direction that the trailer turns."** Turn the steering wheel right to guide the trailer right. This can seem confusing at first, so literally say it in your head: "the space is on my *right*, and I want the trailer to turn *right*, into the space. So I turn *right*." Keep this basic rule in mind and you'll maintain a lot more control over the process.

- **Use help.** This is no time to be proud. Even if you're camping alone, enlist another camper at the campgrounds to give you a hand. A spotter in back can help you streamline the backing-up process, avoid errors, and head off accidents. A safety rule of thumb: the spotter should always stand to the side, never in the path of the rig. When communicating with a helper, say "driver side" or "passenger side" to reference sides of the vehicle. Using "right" and "left" is a sure way to get confused. You can use walkie-talkies or even cell phones to ensure clear communication, or have your helper yell to be sure that you heard the commands.

- **Go slow.** Modest, slow increments can be frustrating, but they're how you maintain total control over the process and stop small obstacles from becoming serious trailer damage.

- **Watch the wheels.** The trailer's wheels are the pivot points for the turn.

TIPS FOR BACKING UP A TRAVEL TRAILER CONTINUED

Here's a graphic step-by-step description of backing a trailer smoothly into a campsite spot.

1. Position the vehicle so the front of the trailer's wheels are just about even with the edge of the site space. Be sure to leave a few feet between the border of the site and the rig (the spacing is different than, for instance, parking at a curb). You can give yourself a bit of a head start by making a shallow "S" motion as your approach the site. Turn slightly away from the site as you come to a stop to prepare for backing up.

2. Cock the trailer by turning the wheel away from the site and the direction you want the trailer to go ultimately, *before* you begin backing up. Once you start the process, slowly unwind the steering ("unsteering") in the other direction.

3. As you proceed, stop a couple of times and check all around the vehicle. As the trailer enters the site space, check the front of the tow vehicle, which will now be straightening and could hit obstacles or vehicles opposite the site.

4. Carefully straighten the tow vehicle. You should wind up driving straight back into the space—if you're cockeyed, *don't* attempt to correct by steering back and forth in small increments. Pull out entirely, take a lap, and try again.

4

CAMPER INTERIOR AND DÉCOR

Wood walls, like the ones that grace this campsite stunner, can be a wonderful camper option. Luan plywood is light and pliable but also has a handsome surface that can hold its own with painted surfaces when finished natural. Wood veneers can be fastened over existing vinyl walls to create a rustic look.

Working on the interior of your camper involves both the practical and the aesthetic. This is your last line of defense for detecting and fixing water damage and other problems, but it is also your opportunity to inject some personality and style into your camper and put your own signature on it. That's why working inside the camper is usually where all the fun happens.

Interior modifications are often the lowest risk and least expensive changes you can make. Because the floor space is relatively limited, you can often choose upscale surface options (as long as they make sense for a structure usually in motion) because you don't need to purchase a lot of material. Be gutsy and don't hesitate to experiment! It's usually easy to reverse any changes you make to the interior.

Any camper renovation or remodeling starts at the top and works down. There's a practical reason for this succession: any water damage likely began on the top or sides of the structure. Fixing the source of a leak takes precedence over fixing subsequent damage from the water infiltration.

WALLS AND CEILINGS

The structure of your camper's walls and ceiling may seem hopelessly complex and daunting to attack during a rehab, but they are in reality exceedingly simple, and easy to rebuild when necessary. And the older your camper, the more it just might be necessary.

Let's start with the difference between aluminum-sided and fiberglass-sided units. If you're rocking an aluminum travel trailer, the walls will have wood studs and the ceiling will have wood joists just like your home. The difference is, the studs will usually be 2 × 2s, while the joists will often be 2 × 4s (depending on the make and model—some feature trusses to create a slightly arced roof). The size of the members can vary depending on your particular camper's manufacturer and on its age. In fact, the framing members in a vintage camper may be actual size rather than nominal size, but the basic type of construction is standard. The studs form the skeleton, the outside skin is attached directly to the outside edge of the studs, and the wall surface is attached directly to the inside. There may be modest insulation in the stud cavities, but often there is not.

If your trailer is fiberglass, the studs will likely be metal. They'll still be thinner than standard house framing but won't be susceptible to rot. However, wall cavities on older fiberglass campers are possible hiding places for vermin, a problem that is alleviated by removing the interior wall surface and cleaning out the cavities.

HOW TO REPAIR WALL WATER DAMAGE

One of the most common types of damage to older trailers is water infiltration in the walls. The real problem is that by the time the water lets its presence be known on the wall surface, it has usually lurked inside the wall for quite some time. That translates to big, unpleasant surprises when you open up a water-damaged wall. Take it one small step it at a time and you might find that the damage wasn't really as difficult to repair as it at first appeared. In any case, wear a dust mask or respirator,

WHAT YOU'LL NEED

- ☐ Heavy duty work gloves
- ☐ Respirator rated for use with mold
- ☐ Eye and ear protection
- ☐ Awl
- ☐ Hammer
- ☐ Jigsaw (optional)
- ☐ Power drill and bits
- ☐ Oscillating saw
- ☐ Construction adhesive

heavy-duty work gloves, and safety glasses whenever you dealing with water damage in a camper.

1 Cut away the wall surface. It's usually best to remove an entire wall panel if only a small part of the panel shows damage. By opening a large section of the wall, you can get a clear idea of how far the damage extends and make everything more accessible.

NOTE: Because corner seams are common sites of water infiltration, it's smart to remove both panels that join in the corner so that you have access to the entire area.

2 Remove and discard any insulation. Wear a long-sleeve shirt, work pants, and boots for this process, because the fiberglass strands can cause itching and allergic reactions. Wear safety glasses and a dust mask or respirator because the same strands are just as bad for your lungs as they are for your eyes.

A small leak in a camper's exterior seams can lead to big problems, and it's hard to tell without opening things up—a single spot of water damage on an interior wall could be hiding extensive rot.

3 Assess the state of the wood studs. Prepare to remove rotted sections by bracing around them.

4 Cut out rotted sections using a reciprocating saw or oscillating saw (excellent for severing any fasteners that hold the skin to the outside of the studs). Support cut studs by sistering a new stud next to it, toenailing it in place to the sole and top plates and to the good wood that is left from the original stud.

NOTE: Never sister good wood to rotted sections; rot can migrate, contaminating and ruining the new member.

5 Make sure the leak has been repaired prior to closing the wall. Clean the wall cavity and ensure that there is no remaining moisture.

6 Install new insulation in the cavity. Coat the stud edges with construction adhesive and enclose the wall with a new wall panel cut to fit the opening. Screw it in place and repaint as necessary.

INSULATING CAMPER WALLS

It doesn't matter whether you're planning on camping in winter or not: it only makes good sense to insulate your camper's walls. The construction of a camper basically makes it a heat- and cold-conducting box. So it's not only naturally chilly on cold nights and during the fall and winter, but it also gets mega hot in direct sun exposure or any time the temperature outside dances around triple digits.

Insulating the walls—especially during an overall rehab or remodeling in which you remove the wall surfaces—is easy. The more difficult part is deciding on what to use for insulation.

- **FIBERGLASS BATTS.** This itchy, floppy form of insulation is difficult and unpleasant to install, but it can easily be stuffed into the cramped confines of a camper's wall cavities, and the r-value (a measure of the material's resistance to heat transfer) is a hefty 3.2 per inch. The problem? Compacting the insulation diminishes the r-value, and although the standard batt is 3½ inches thick, the average wall cavity in a camper is 2 inches deep. For this and other reasons, fiberglass batting is rarely used to insulate campers.

- **POLYSTYRENE FOAM BOARD.** Easily identifiable by its pink color, this solid board product is easy to cut, can be jammed into odd-size cavities, and comes in 1-inch thicknesses perfect for use in a camper's wall cavities. Unfortunately, the r-value can't match even compacted batt insulation. That's why most people install multiple layers of board insulation.

- **POLYISOCYANURATE ("POLYISO") BOARD.** This is the latest in insulation technology. This closed-cell rigid foam board product features a high r-value—typically around 6 per inch of thickness. The drawback to this option is the expense. Expect to pay more than $30 for a 4 × 8-foot sheet. Polyiso board is also susceptible to shrinkage over time. That's why it's recommended that you tape the board in place against the studs, using insulation tape, to prevent any airflow gaps.

The r-value of any insulation is negated to some degree by cold or hot air migrating through gaps. That's why it's just as important as the insulation itself to make sure there are no air leaks that will counteract the benefit. Check weather stripping and seals around doors, windows, skylights, and vents, and replace as necessary. Fix or replace windows that are skewed in their openings, have cracks, or don't close tightly.

DRESSING UP WALLS AND CEILINGS

The colors, patterns, and textures of your camper's walls usually set the tone for the entire decor. A fresh surface can instantaneously change the interior look from drab and dreary to sparkling. Glampers usually look at wall surfaces as the best place to start decorating their *pied à terre* in a box. How you resurface those walls depends on what they're made of.

Although the color scheme may be a bit bland, vinyl walls like these can easily be painted to bring new life to the camper. They are essentially a blank canvas for any adventurous glamper builder.

VINYL

From the 1970s onward, vinyl walls were commonly used as interior wall cladding on camper trailers of all sizes. The material is inexpensive, flexible, durable, resistant to moisture and structural stresses, and extremely easy to clean. Problem is, most vinyl surfaces are anything but beautiful. A lot of glampers refer to stock vinyl camper walls as the "dentist office" look. They can be a little tricky to paint, but painting is often the best and easiest solution to beautify vinyl walls. The trick is getting the paint to actually bond to the surface of the vinyl. Some simple prep will ensure an eye-catching surface that stays beautiful over the long run.

1 Use a 1:1 mixture of white vinegar and warm water to wash down the walls you'll be painting. You can also use a degreasing cleaner or other strong cleaning product meant for use on vinyl. Whatever you use, make sure the walls are absolutely clean before you proceed. Dry the walls completely.

2 A light sanding is your opportunity to smooth out any existing surface texture while creating "tooth" that will hold primer and paint to the surface of the walls. Wearing a dust mask, use 100-grit paper with a sanding block and don't go crazy. Clean up afterward with a tack cloth until the wall and surrounding area are dust free.

3 Don't attempt to paint a vinyl wall with an all-in-one, paint-and-primer product. Laying down a base of a quality bonding-sealing primer is key to the best-looking paint job possible (and one that won't peel or degrade over time).

4 Again, given how close any viewer will be to the surface of your camper's walls, use the best paint you can buy as a top coat. Paint is not a place to scrimp on the rehab. The small coverage area will limit what you have to spend, and the result will be well worth the investment.

FAUX WOOD

Fake wood paneling is also a common older and not-so-old camper wall surface. The material is inexpensive and easy to clean. If any section of paneling is damaged, it's a simple fix to remove a given panel and replace it. But the "wood" graining is obviously fake and the look is dated—in a bad way.

Faux wood or wood veneer—like the type used in this trailer—doesn't have to be cheesy (although older versions often are). You'll find new veneer products that are much more convincing, including versions that feature distinctive graining patterns like the surfaces in this example.

Use the same process—and especially the same painting products—to paint old wood paneling as you would a vinyl wall. Here again, it's essential that the surface be absolutely clean and dry before you begin priming and painting.

PLYWOOD

Some vintage trailers, such as teardrops and smaller travel trailers, were constructed with plywood interior walls and ceilings. Rehabbing these surfaces entails cutting out and replacing any rotted or damaged wood sections, filling the gaps with wood putty or similar sealant, sanding everything smooth, and priming and painting as you would any wood surface. However, plywood can also be an eye-catching visual left unpainted, as long as it's the right type of plywood.

Luan plywood is commonly used as a wall-surface replacement material in camper rehabs because it's low cost, thin (commonly ¼ inch but sometime offered ⅛ inch thick), pliable, and easy to work with. The biggest challenge to working with Luan plywood is cutting it, because the cut edge is prone to splintering. To avoid this, the cutline is often pre-scored with a utility knife, cut slowly with a fine-tooth crosscut blade, and cut with the cutline taped over with painter's tape. Once in place, the surface is very smooth and—to many people—attractive enough to be stained or finished natural. But the plywood also takes paint well, and can be primed and painted as any wood surface would be.

Dated grooved wood paneling is common in smaller vintage trailers.

REAL WOOD

Wood walls can create a substantial look in the inside of a trailer. There are so many varieties of wood to choose from that there's an appearance for every taste. Select from sophisticated hardwoods like ipe or mahogany (before you choke on the price tag, remember that the wonderful thing about rehabbing a camper is the small amount of remodeling materials you'll actually use) to

Cedar boards installed horizontally create a unique ranch bunkhouse look in this truck camper. It's a distinctive look and one that sets the interior apart from your run-of-the-mill camper. *Courtesy Capri Camper*

plainer, more common looks like walnut, cherry, or even oak. The options increase with stains; you can go natural, light, dark, and even pickled or whitened.

The format of the wood can also radically affect the perception of the surface. Use traditional tongue-and-groove wood paneling for a very rustic or "lodge" appeal. Go more modern or contemporary with short wood planks nailed to the studs vertically. Whatever style the wood, keep in mind that the thickness of the wood is going to cut into the interior space. Use wood on all the walls and you'll lose a few inches of floor space. That may not seem like a lot, but it can have an impact on the interior of a small camper trailer or truck trailer.

ALUMINUM

In rare cases, like older Airstream trailers, you may want to paint interior metal surfaces. The majority of aluminum trailer owners polish bare walls. Although most people consider polished aluminum a sophisticated look, you may decide maintaining the polished appearance is too much hassle. In that case, follow these instructions to paint interior aluminum walls.

1   Clean the wall with a cleaner-degreaser meant for aluminum, following the directions on the bottle. Rinse the surface thoroughly with distilled water, and then dry it completely.

2   Wearing a dust mask, use fine-grit sandpaper to rough up the surface and remove any protective clear coat that might have been applied. Clean up afterward with a tack cloth until the wall and surrounding area are dust free.

3   Brush or spray the wall with aluminum oxide primer, following the instructions on the can. Make sure that you allow appropriate time for the primer to dry.

4   Sand the primed surface lightly with 220-grit sandpaper and a sanding block. You just want to remove any imperfections and slightly rough up the surface of the primer to receive the top coat. Clean up afterward with a tack cloth until the wall and surrounding area are dust free.

5   Brush or spray a top coat of epoxy paint labeled for use on aluminum, following the instructions on the can closely, and allow 48 hours for the paint to cure before touching the surface.

The sleek ceiling in this Airstream bedroom is proof positive that aluminum interior surfaces can be simply stunning and are a timeless look. The metal surface complements all the other surfaces in the space and is an eye-catching feature on its own.

CAMPER PAINTING TIPS

In the small space of a camper's interior, minor imperfections are magnified. Take the time to properly prep interior walls and the ceiling prior to painting. If you're not absolutely sure of your cut-in skills, or have little faith in your steady hand, tape cut-in lines with painter's tape.

The vast majority of new camper trailers are manufactured with bland neutral color schemes, because earth tones hide dirt, aren't challenging to the eye, and tend to appeal to the largest audience. But if you're a glamper, be fearless in your choice of colors.

The confines of any camper—even larger fifth wheels—are natural candidates for light, bright colors. Pure white, sky blue, yellow, or violet will all increase the sense of space. Complementary color schemes will be especially effective—classic combos include blue and orange, or purple and yellow, but you can find your own favorites on the color wheel. Just play it safe and use complements of the exact same shade (amount of white in the color). Monochromatic schemes are also effective inside a camper. Whether it's all white, pure pale lavender, or light forest green, monochromatic interiors are generally restful to the eyes.

Although you can certainly paint the ceiling as part of any color scheme, it's often wisest to leave your camper ceiling bright white. That creates the illusion of headroom and will do justice to any colors that you use in the rest of the interior.

THE PAINT ALTERNATIVE

Wallpaper is an option for rehabbing your camper, but it's a less-than-perfect one. If there is existing wallpaper, that material was most likely bonded to the wall surface in a controlled process during manufacture, rather than being applied after the camper was built. That means the existing paper will be harder to remove than wallpaper in a home would be.

Existing painted wall surfaces will need to be properly prepared because obviously there is more flex and give in camper walls than in the walls of a home. But the more important consideration is the actual type of wallpaper you use. In general, it's best to hang thick vinyl wallpaper in a camper because of the potential for moisture in the environment. Beyond the concern about leaks, most campers are not thoroughly vented, and condensation and vapors from cooking, showering, and propane appliances can affect wall coverings more than they would in a house.

THE ACCENT WALL

Want to add an eye-catching design feature to the inside of your camper? Take a page out of the home designer's handbook and consider an accent wall. This is usually a narrow divider wall, or some other modest partition that you paint in a bold, attention-grabbing hue. Think lime green, bright orange, or fire engine red. Because the wall surface area is usually modest, you're not taking much of a risk. If the color wears on you, it's easy enough to quickly paint it white or neutral to match the rest of your interior. But when an accent wall works, it brings an exciting jolt of unexpected color into the space, adding energy and style.

FABULOUS FLOORS

Floors are often the forgotten surfaces in a camper rehab. It's so easy to forget about flooring when you're focusing on stenciling wall surfaces, hanging those handmade curtains you worked so hard on, or sprucing up your cabinets with stunning, fresh countertops. But a new floor can be the icing on the cake of any camper rehab.

Before you lay a new floor, it is absolutely essential that you make sure the subfloor surface is sound. Use the opportunity of replacing the flooring to inspect and repair any sections of rot or other damage to the subfloor. You'll be making the whole camper structure more secure.

Pickled wood floors? Nope, vinyl planks. Vinyl floor surfaces have come a long way, and the appearances now convincingly mimic all kinds of wood, stone, and tile. Regardless of the look, the flooring is durable and long-lasting.

HOW TO REPLACE ROTTED SUBFLOOR

The biggest mistake camper rehabbers make when trying to fix a rotted section of subfloor is underestimating how big an area may be affected. If you're going to the trouble to remedy rot or subfloor damage, you're tackling a problem that requires a good bit of work. You might as well remedy it so completely that you never have to do it again.

1 Remedy the leak or situation that cause the rot or damage in the first place. Then mark the area you'll be working on with a Sharpie and straightedge, leaving an ample margin around the damaged or rotted subfloor.

WHAT YOU'LL NEED

- ☐ Work gloves
- ☐ Eye and ear protection
- ☐ Sharpie
- ☐ Metal straightedge
- ☐ Circular saw
- ☐ Pry bar (optional)
- ☐ Angle grinder (optional)
- ☐ Measuring tape
- ☐ Utility knife (optional)
- ☐ Reciprocating saw (optional)
- ☐ Power drill and bits
- ☐ Stainless-steel screws

2 Remove the flooring over the damaged area. Remove fixtures such as cabinets that sit over any section of the affected area. Keep in mind that you want clear access not only to remove damage but also to maneuver the new subfloor patch into place.

NOTE: *This is an excellent time to upgrade flooring throughout the camper.*

3 Clean up the area to clearly assess how far the damage has spread. Plan the removal of the affected section. Straight cuts are always better, because they make for tighter fits of the new patch material. Use a circular saw to cut out the affected area. You may need to pry sections loose where they've been fastened to floor joists.

OPTIONAL: Cut away rotted bolts or those you can't access from underneath the trailer, and any rusted-out fasteners, with an angle grinder. Plan on replacing the bolts to properly secure the floor.

4 Remove all the debris and rotted wood before continuing and assess the floor joists running under the affected area. Do they have any areas of rot or damage? If so, cut out and replace the affected joists at this point. Add the insulation at this point if you are insulating the floor.

5 Measure carefully and cut a subfloor patch from identical material. Keep in mind that vintage campers may have used actual size plywood as the floor base. Trying to patch with nominal-size equivalent will create an uneven surface. You can either add a thin substrate (such as wood veneer sheet) sandwiched to the new patch or shim or otherwise account for the difference in thickness. Fasten down the subfloor with stainless-steel screws.

6 Replace the top flooring. Depending on where the patch falls and what fixtures or furnishings sit on top, you'll need to either use matching floor to blend the patched area into the rest of the floor or use a different material and a transition strip. Replace all the furnishings or fixtures over the patch.

Choosing the best flooring for your camper is about much more than just what tickles your fancy and your toes. The ideal floor will be long lasting, attractive, inexpensive, and easy to clean. Thankfully, you'll find lots of options that fit those criteria.

VINYL

This synthetic flooring is available in sheet, planks, and tiles. Sheet vinyl flooring can be a bit difficult to work with in the confines of a camper, unless you've gutted the camper for a complete rebuild. Should you want to try the more challenging sheet format (upside: no seams), warm up the sheet before laying it to make the material as workable as possible. Also consult the manufacturer and talk to the retailer about specific aspects of installing sheet vinyl in a camper. Spoiler alert—it's a little unwieldy but completely doable. However, most pros advise against gluing the flooring to the subfloor and will recommend alternatives such as edge stapling.

Flexible vinyl planks are the easier, less frustrating option. Their simple installation is why they are quickly becoming the most popular format of vinyl flooring. They basically just lay on top of the floor and snap together to create a relatively watertight surface. You can also opt for super easy peel-and-stick vinyl tiles. They're the paint-by-numbers option that are just dry laid to determine position, and then stuck in place once the backing is peeled off. The tiles do, however, have a tendency to peel up over time and the gaps between tiles can become wider and more apparent with the continual flexing of a camper's floor. They also loosen in temperature extremes, so they are not ideal in a vacation getaway that can pass through deserts.

The main reason for vinyl flooring's popularity is because the surface can be molded into an astounding number of textures and copycat appearances. Styles range from simple, mono-colored sheets, to vinyl planks that look convincingly like stone, to tiles with totally unique relief textures. The material itself is durable, easy to clean, and competitively priced.

LAMINATE

Like vinyl, laminate flooring is a chameleon. Snap-lock versions of laminate plank flooring are available in realistic approximations of stone, a variety of hard and softwoods, and ceramic tiles. This flooring has enough flexibility to absorb the various stresses a camper encounters. Laminate planks are also easy to work with and install and are competitively priced, especially if you have

a smaller trailer with a small amount of square footage to cover. Laminate is reasonably durable, although deep scratches can compromise the flooring. That said, it's easy to remove and replace a damaged laminate plank.

One caveat, however, about laminate flooring: beware of versions containing formaldehyde. This has been a problem with flooring from China, and the EPA subsequently recommended that anyone buying laminate flooring check that the product is stamped or labeled that it is in compliance with the California Air Resources Board's Airborne Toxics Control Measures (CARB ATCMs).

LINOLEUM

This healthy, earth-friendly option has been around forever and a day and is still just as resilient, cleanable, and long lasting as it always was. Modern linoleum is mostly sold under the name "marmoleum" and is available in a thick sheet product that is difficult to maneuver and work with in a small space like a camper trailer. But it is also sold in more popular "click" tiles. The tiles are manufactured of strand board—or other substrate— topped with the linoleum. The tiles or planks simply click together, making installation very easy. Marmoleum comes in many different surfaces appearances, from solid colors and patterns to imitations of wood.

CARPET

Carpet remains an immensely popular choice for camper floors, both new and old, but the material is actually less than ideal for this application. Although it is perhaps the most comfortable surface for bare feet, it is also a magnet for dirt in a structure that's often surrounded by nothing but. Carpet, especially really luxurious deep-pile versions, traps allergens and contaminants that can significantly deteriorate indoor air quality. New carpeting commonly off-gasses vapors that smell bad and can impact respiratory health. The wrong carpet can retain moisture from spills or general condensation, which can in turn lead to mold conditions. Carpet also wears; if you use your camper a lot with active family members, be prepared to replace the carpet in a few years.

Traditional-appearance laminate flooring blends well with earth-tone interiors and other wood surfaces, as it does in this dinette area. Newer laminates are more durable and more realistic in appearance than early versions.

A favorite among manufacturers from the 1970s onward, plain beige carpet is certainly a comfortable surface underfoot, but it tends to capture moisture and dirt.

All that said, the small square footage of most campers makes finding and purchasing a luxury remnant a snap. Carpet in campers is installed in exactly the same way—with tack strips and stretching—as it is in a home. If that seems like too involved a process for your particular camper renovation, you can always turn to the option of press-and-stick carpet tiles. You'll find these in various naps and many different colors and patterns. The downside to the ease of installation is that there are minute gaps between each tile, potential avenues for water infiltration.

WOOD

Although you can install wood planks, strips, or squares in a camper, it's not usually a practical choice. The natural bouncing and flexing a trailer endures will tend to separate planks or strips at their joints, and the temperature extremes to which many trailers are exposed can cause undue expansion and contraction in wood floors. All that movement can, in some cases, lead to separation and buckling.

However, if you're rocking an insulated camper and you want an upscale look (and you've instituted a no-shoes rule), wood can be a dynamic choice. Choose from an amazing diversity of grain patterns and natural shades. Or select a stain for just the look that suits you and your camper best.

WHAT TO AVOID

Some flooring options just aren't right for a camper. For instance, hard tiles are bound to separate along grout lines, opening up avenues for water infiltration—not to mention just looking awful. It's why stone or ceramic tiles are not a good idea for camper flooring. An industrial look such as bare metal would be a poor choice as well, because it would be incredibly uncomfortable underfoot.

Real wood floors can be an excellent choice for an upscale, streamlined, contemporary camper interior.

FURNISHINGS

As important as bringing new life to the camper's skin or updating the propane system may be, rehabbing interior furnishings is where the big bang for your buck lies. If you've purchased a camper trailer with more than a decade of hard outdoor adventures under its belt, the furnishings are likely showing their age and then some. Or it may be that you prefer a different floor plan than the one the manufacturer intended. Whatever the reason, this is the part of a camper rehab project where you can really let your imagination run.

There are three ways to breathe new life into your camper's furnishings: spruce up what's there, replace with RV furniture intended for use in traveling homes, or replace with home furnishings adapted to the purpose.

COUCHES AND LOVESEATS

Not every camper actually has a loveseat or sofa, but the ones that do enjoy some of the most comfortable seating a traveling home can include. If you're working with a typical built-in bench seat with modest cushions, you can certainly reupholster the cushions and call it a day. But often, the

cushions are shot, the backrest is torture, and the entire structure doesn't fit into your rehab plans. Even if you have a sofa in place, chances are it's looking a little long in the tooth. Unfortunately, the reality is that reupholstering a camper couch can be as expensive as replacing it, depending on the material you choose and the company that is doing the work. Upgrading to an aftermarket RV sofa is a way to introduce a fresh new look and a lot of luxury.

When it comes to heavy, large, padded and upholstered furniture, the safest strategy is always to replace like with like. Look to match the measurements of a new piece as closely as possible to what's already there. Changing sofa sizes can make an aisle unpassable, or conversely leave large areas of blank wall next to an undersized unit. You can also exploit the opportunity of replacing an existing sofa or loveseat to install a unit with added functions. These days, most RV sofas and loveseats serve dual purposes—comfy seating at all times, and an extra bunk when you need it.

- **JACK-KNIFE COUCH.** It looks like an ordinary sofa, but grab a hidden handle and give a yank, and the couch back and seat come forward and flatten into a bed. It's meant to be used lengthwise, which can be awfully handy in a narrow camper where a pullout sleeper sofa would not fit. Jack-knife couches are an inexpensive replacement for older static couches. However, they are rarely a super comfortable bed and best used as sleeping quarters on an occasional basis. You can make the experience more comfortable by using a foam mattress topper, but no matter what, a tall person is going to find the experience of sleeping on a jack-knife couch less than ideal.

- **PULLOUT SLEEPER SOFA.** Just like a sleeper sofa in your home, this couch conceals a bed under the seat cushions. You pull it out, unfolding a metal support structure. The bed is perpendicular to the width of the sofa, providing much more room for sleeping than a jack-knife model would. However, be absolutely sure that you have the space in your camper to fully pull out the bed—otherwise, the advantage is wasted and the sleeping function will be unusable. It's also worth considering that the weight of a sleeper sofa is considerable. The more weight you add in the camper, the harder the towing will be and the worse the fuel economy. Mattress quality is key in sleeper sofas. Lower-priced units will have thin, feeble foam mattresses that make for unsatisfying sleep and back and joint aches. You can upgrade the mattress or buy a sofa with a higher quality mattress to start with. If the unit will be used often for sleeping, either will be a good investment. (For more on camper mattresses, see page 52.)

- **AIR-MATTRESS SLEEPER SOFA.** These are the relative newcomers to campers and RVs. They are an alternative to the traditional sleeper sofa and feature a more lightweight mattress and support structure because both are inflatable. These are also more comfortable than most pullout sleeper sofas because there are not metal bars to disrupt sleep and create body aches. Weight savings are a bonus with this style of sofa.

- **HOME SOFAS.** There's nothing stopping you from installing a standard home sofa or loveseat in place of your camper unit. Just keep in mind that the sofa must be secured in place, and it must work in the confines of the camper and the space occupied by your original camper sofa.

One factor you can influence, however, is access. Movement around camper beds is often impeded by cabinets and closets. If you don't bring a lot of clothes with you on your camping trips—or if all the clothes you do bring can be folded—you may be able to completely remove closets without missing the storage space.

The bigger issue is the bed's mattress. Most stock mattresses, and certainly those included on older campers, are little more than a foam pad. If you use your camper frequently or just value your sleep, replacing the mattress will be high on your to-do list. Thankfully, you'll find tons of replacement options on the market. Manufacturers offer everything from inexpensive 4-inch-thick foam units that are simple replacements for a guest bed to master suite luxury memory foam mattresses with gel tops. Prices range from less than $100 for a bargain-basement model to $700 for a top-of-the-line memory foam option. You'll find information on common RV mattress sizes on page 52.

BEDS

One of the primary advantages of taking a camper with you on your wilderness vacations is that you have something much more comfortable to sleep on than a thin mat, a sleeping bag, and the bottom of a tent. Unfortunately, depending on the camper, the size of the bed, and the mattress, it may not be a whole lot more comfortable.

It's usually difficult to completely change the actual bed size or orientation. As the largest flat surface in most campers, the bed is situated before any other part of the floor plan. Unless you're willing to totally redesign the overall floor plan, the chances are that you'll be dealing with the existing dimensions of the bed.

The ideal primary bed in a camper is much like this one: easy to walk around, equipped with surfaces for reading materials, eyeglasses, and a glass of water or coffee, and within reach of electrical outlets and light sources.

LIGHTING

Updating camper lighting fixtures is an easy, quick way to put your own stamp on the interior design while upgrading the illumination and task lighting inside the camper. In most cases, it makes sense to have a mixture of ambient (general) light sources—such as an overhead dome light in the center of the trailer— and specific task lighting, like reading lights on the bed's headboard.

Before buying or replacing any lighting fixtures, assess your needs and usage, and develop an overall lighting plan. It may become apparent that you want or need fixtures where there currently aren't any. Wiring in new fixtures can be a major project. Unless you're well versed in RV electrical systems, you may want to leave installing brand-new fixtures to your local RV repair and customization professional.

Any time you swap out a camper lighting fixture, make sure the new fixture is meant for use in a camper trailer or RV. It's not just a matter of being rugged enough to survive countless miles of travel; light fixtures in campers are usually wired into the 12-volt, direct-current circuit. You should also strongly consider converting to LED lights on the inside of the camper. They use less energy, provide a clean, white light that is better for reading and detail work, and last much longer than incandescents.

Beyond function, match the form to your camper's interior design. Pick brass finishes for a traditional vintage travel trailer that features dark wood and neutral fabrics. Opt for brushed nickel or chrome in a camper full of glistening white surfaces or sparkling with bright, fun colors.

Don't stop at the interior. The "porch" lights on the outside of the trailer can set the mood for relaxing with a drink outside on a summer's eve. You can update exterior camper lights with like for like, but you might consider directional lights that give you more control over exterior illumination.

ACCENTS and FUN TOUCHES

Dressing up whatever changes you make inside your camper is the icing on the interior's cake. Cake may be darn delicious, but it always looks even more delicious covered in shiny icing! The small decorative touches you add don't necessarily make the structure any better, but they will improve the atmosphere, will give you a chance to put your own stamp on your camper, and are easy and inexpensive.

WINDOW TREATMENTS

Window coverings afford you privacy when you're camping in a crowded campsite with trailers on either side of you—or if you'd just prefer the bears and moose don't get a peek inside. They can also add powerful decorative elements. If you know your way around a sewing machine, pick out a custom fabric and really scrawl your signature across the interior. Because they are such small real estate visually, curtains are a wonderful place to be a little daring; bold colors and vibrant, fun patterns are worth trying. You can also add touches like lace hems and pleats. However, always keep in mind that curtains are meant to be functional. Grommet holes are often the easiest and best solution for mounting the curtains.

If you don't happen to have any skill with a sewing machine, don't fret. You'll find a world of curtain options at retail. Some RV suppliers offer curtains made especially for camper trailer windows (usually made of thick, opaque material, to be used as total privacy curtains). These tend toward neutral colors with plain shapes and styles to fit the widest range of interior styles, but they are usually reasonably priced and well made.

Whether you're custom sewing your curtains or buying prefab versions, always consider how they'll be mounted and secured.

Matching window treatments to established colors—like the royal blue of these curtains that coordinate perfectly with the stripes in the dinette seating—is the easiest way to ensure an eye-pleasing look.

Blinds can be a great solution for windows where you want to allow some illumination in, but don't want direct, blinding sunlight in the middle of the day.

Tieback straps or hooks are small decorative elements themselves but should be first and foremost easy to use. Valances traditionally match the fabric, color, and pattern of the curtains themselves. But if you have retrofitted decorative slide curtain rods, show them off. Eliminating valances can save you money, time, and effort.

SHADES AND BLINDS

Shades or blinds are simpler window-covering options that are more about function than style. If privacy and shade are key to where and how you camp, light-blocking black-out shades or blinds may be a better option than curtains. (Although blinds are a natural partner to curtains and nothing says you can't have both!) These can be super effective options for anyone who regularly camps in very hot, dry areas or in sun-drenched, exposed campground lots. Darkening the interior of the camper during the day can go far to keeping it cool.

The challenge of retrofitting shades or blinds to a used trailer's windows—and especially vintage windows—is proper sizing. Chances are that you won't find shades or blinds off the rack. However, you'll find many sources for custom blinds or shades made to fit your windows. Mounting them entails nothing more than aligning, leveling, and screwing them in place.

FABRIC TOUCHES

One of the most versatile strategies for decorating the interior of a camper with accents that can be quickly, easily, and inexpensively changed is to splash textiles around the space. Bedding can be a way to introduce visual textures that soften some of the hard edges common to camper interior materials. The right bedding not only adds pattern, color, and texture but also makes sleeping a lot more comfortable. That's why you shouldn't hesitate to splurge on a bed cover and pillowcases that add visual excitement or fun to the space—particularly if the bedroom is not separated from the rest of the interior.

Throws or cushion slipcovers are also excellent, low-cost ways to introduce vibrant visuals into the interior. There are many fun and wild options. Choose fabrics that capture the spirit you're going for and bring a dash of life and interest to the space.

Area rugs help reinforce the tone of your decor. A hooked, multicolor throw rug can be ideal for adding visual variety to a country interior, while a Berber runner might be more fitting for a sophisticated style used inside a vintage Airstream.

CANDLES AND STRING LIGHTS

These decorative accents are not only lots of fun on a camping trip, but they also have a functional side. Candles can be fallback lighting for when your batteries are low and you're not hooked up to a shoreline or have a generator at your disposal (or just don't want to deal with the noise and smell). Outdoor string lights bring an undeniably festive atmosphere to the sitting area right outside the door of your camper. Buy solar-powered versions that charge up during the day and last most of the night.

LUXURY ACCENTS

You'll find a host of luxury retrofits at RV suppliers. For instance, hardwood bar racks that can be attached to the wall next to a kitchen to securely hold stem glasses and tumblers are a wonderful way to bring delicate glassware along on your outdoor adventures. The glasses themselves are elegant visuals. You can pick a cabinet add-on like a pullout wine drawer, to keep your favorite bottles close at hand.

CABINETS

Cabinets and closets in most campers are fairly low quality. Not only is it cheaper to build these structures with MDF and wood veneer or laminate rather than real wood, but it's also much lighter (vintage campers often feature cabinets made from thin plywood). Although you can certainly replace camper cabinets, it's an easy project to reinforce the cabinets as necessary and cover them with a coat of paint for a fresh new look. This is a great way to refresh the look of the interior and put your own stamp on it in the process. You don't have to limit yourself to simply painting the cabinets. You can stencil designs on the doors, go two-tone with doors in different colors from the cabinet bodies, or use special painting techniques like sponging to create a wholly unique look.

HOW TO PAINT CAMPER CABINETS

It's amazing how a simple change such as painting cabinet bodies and doors can transform the interior of a camper. This is especially true in smaller campers where cabinets and closets dominate the visual impression of the space. Many glamper enthusiasts take the opportunity of painting cabinets to also paint all the interior walls. Whether you do that or not, painting cabinets is an easy project that offers instant gratification.

1 Remove the cabinets if you're rehabbing the entire interior and making some major improvements or repairs. If not, remove the doors and hardware with a screwdriver or power drill, and mask off walls and floors around the cabinets with plastic sheeting and painter's tape.

WHAT YOU'LL NEED

- ☐ Work gloves
- ☐ Eye and ear protection
- ☐ Screwdrivers
- ☐ Power drill and bits
- ☐ Painter's tape
- ☐ Plastic sheeting
- ☐ TSP cleaner or similar
- ☐ Measuring tape
- ☐ Replacement fasteners and brackets (optional)
- ☐ Wood filler or putty (optional)
- ☐ Putty knife
- ☐ Glue syringe (optional)
- ☐ Wood glue (optional)
- ☐ Clamps
- ☐ Dust mask
- ☐ Sandpaper and sanding sponge
- ☐ Drop cloth
- ☐ Paintbrush
- ☐ Stain-blocking primer-sealer
- ☐ Paint
- ☐ Tack cloth

2 Clean the cabinets thoroughly with a TSP-type cleaner (you can find handy-to-use spray cleaners labeled as "TSP Substitute" for this purpose). Let them dry completely before proceeding.

3 Reinforce the cabinets as necessary. If the structure is out of square (measure diagonals to determine this), or any walls or parts of the cabinet are loose, tighten or replace screws and other fasteners. Add metal L brackets in the corners, measuring the diagonals after you're done to ensure the cabinets are square. Fix any separations in door miter joints.

4 Fill any holes or cracks with wood filler. Where the laminate is separating from the underlying MDF, use a glue syringe to inject wood glue underneath the laminate, roll it entirely flat, and clamp it until it dries. If there are missing sections of laminate, fill the depressions with wood filler, level it with the surrounding surface, and sand everything smooth when all the filler is dry.

5 Lay down a drop cloth. Prime the cabinets with a stain-blocking primer-sealer and let dry. Wearing a dust mask, sand any rough spots with a sanding sponge or fine-grit sandpaper. Clean up with a tack cloth.

6 Paint the cabinets with the enamel top coat of your choice. Use a quality paint and apply thin coats (it's better to use two or more thin coats than one thick coat). Reassemble the cabinets when dry.

If your cabinets are completely beat up, with stripped screws, contact damage, cracking, or moisture swelling in the MDF panels, it may be wise to replace them. It's not a challenge to use existing cabinet panels as templates to cut new MDF panels for cabinet boxes. You can buy aftermarket wood doors or make your own if you have a basic woodworking setup at home. However, be sure to seal all the edges of any MDF. Use a clear-coat sealant to avoid moisture swelling, a common problem in MDF camper cabinet bodies.

TRIMS

Depending on the age and style of your cabinets, any exposed edges may be covered with plastic trim. The most common type is T-trim, which has a flat or slightly arced surface and a perpendicular leg that sits in an edge channel, holding the trim securely in place. You can paint your existing plastic trim, but the trim does not take paint well, and the paint may flake over time. Replacement T-trim is available in several different colors. It is inexpensive and easy to install, and provides the icing on the cake to rehabbed cabinets. Simply pull out the old trim, and tap the new trim into place with a rubber or wood mallet. Trim off the end and edge excess with a new razor blade, and the cabinets will look like they just arrived from the factory.

COUNTERS

Camper countertops take a lot of abuse. They have to be durable, and yet they should be as lightweight as possible. If your countertops are so beat up that they detract from the rest of the interior, replacing them may be the way to go. It's wise not to expect the same wide selection of options you would in redoing a home's kitchen. It simply doesn't make sense in most cases to install something like granite or travertine surfaces. Generally, camper counters are Formica or MDF covered with a faux surface.

HOW TO REPLACE A COUNTER

Camper counters are often subject to a lot of abuse. Countertops and dinette tabletops often show an older camper's age more than other surfaces in the interior. When these are sufficiently dinged up and timeworn, no amount of cleaning will make them sparkle and seem new.

It may be that water infiltrated the surface over time, as you did the dishes or set fluids on the counter. It could just be one too many heavy objects dropped on the surface, or the simple reality of being a plain flat surface in structure that is so often in motion and flexing with every bump in the road.

Whatever the case, there may well come a time when you need to replace your camper's counters (and it may be first on the to-do list for that older canned ham model you just bought). Although it can seem daunting, the process is actually not technically difficult. With a bit of accurate measurement and the right tools, the job won't take you more than a few hours over the weekend.

WHAT YOU'LL NEED

- ☐ Work gloves
- ☐ Eye and ear protection
- ☐ Screwdrivers
- ☐ Slip-joint pliers
- ☐ Wrenches
- ☐ Utility knife
- ☐ Pry bar
- ☐ Power drill and bits
- ☐ Stainless-steel screws
- ☐ Construction adhesive
- ☐ Router
- ☐ Jigsaw
- ☐ Laminate
- ☐ 1½" birch plywood
- ☐ Silicone caulk

1 **TOP:** Remove the doors and drawers to the base cabinets. Disconnect the sink drain and water hookups, if there is a sink in the counter. Remove the sink fixtures from their mounting holes and set them aside.

2 **MIDDLE:** Unbolt any mounting bolts holding the sink in place, and slice the caulking seal between the sink and the counter. Lift the sink out of the counter and set aside.

3 **BOTTOM:** Remove any undercounter appliances, such as the refrigerator, here. However, if your refrigerator is a propane model, you'll need to hire a plumber unless you are entirely comfortable working with gas hookups.

4 **TOP:** If there is a range or cooktop set into the counter, you'll need to remove it prior to replacing the counter. Disconnect all hookups to the burners, and then unscrew the case or mounting frame from the counter (inset) and pull out the cooktop out.

5 **MIDDLE:** Cut any caulking seal between the counter and any backsplash.

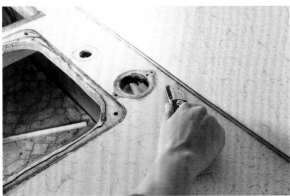

6 **BOTTOM:** Unscrew corner blocks and any other counter fasteners and carefully pry the counter up away from the cabinet frame. Pull the counter out and away from the wall, and remove it entirely.

7 If you have a matching backsplash to your countertop—a common feature in older campers—now is a good time to replace and update the backsplash as well. This is especially important if there has been any water damage on the wall behind the backsplash. Start by removing any trim around the backsplash using a utility knife.

8 Pull the backsplash away from the wall and remove it. Repair any water or other damage to the wall behind the backsplash.

9 **TOP LEFT:** Sand or scrape the top of the cabinet frame to remove all old glue and debris. Wipe the top frame clean and take the opportunity to repair any flaws in the cabinet interior.

10 **TOP RIGHT:** Measure the cabinet box diagonals to ensure the box is square. Install new corner blocks as necessary, coating the corner with construction adhesive before screwing them in place.

11 Cut the new counter using the old as a template (if it is not badly damaged and you haven't altered the cabinet box). Cut a laminate or veneer top and edge banding and apply according to the manufacturer's directions. Cut out any openings needed in the top surface.

NOTE: *For the new counter here, we used 1½" Birch plywood with a laminate top. The plywood edges are handsome enough to leave uncovered.*

12 **ABOVE:** Lay a bead of silicone caulk along the top edge of the frame. Set the new counter in place. Screw it down through the corner blocks.

13 Cut the backsplash surface to fit the space. Spread a ziz-zag bead of construction adhesive on the backsplash wall and firmly press the backsplash into position. Tape it in place until the construction adhesive dries.

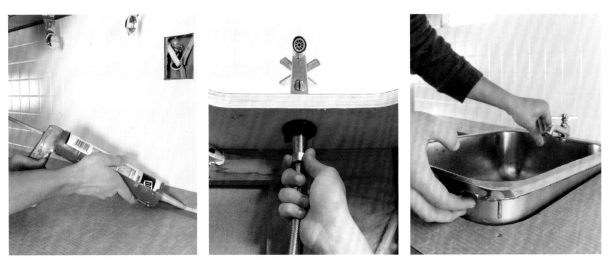

14 Lay a bead of silicone caulk between the counter and backsplash. Replace the fixtures, sink, and stove and secure them to the counter. Hook up the water and propane connections as necessary. Test that the water and stove burners work.

STORAGE ACCESSORIES

No camper rehab would be complete without some handy small organizers that efficiently secure all those little necessities that make life so pleasant on a camping trip. These aftermarket add-ons are designed to stop smaller items from rattling around during travel, and to keep them easy to find and access when you need them.

CABINET ORGANIZERS can be lifesavers. Nobody wants to park at a campsite, ready to relax, only to find that the inside of the camper's cabinets look like a tornado ripped through them. Slide-out bins are handy and easy to install. Door-back spice racks keep spices near at hand and well organized. Cabinet bars are an essential for every cabinet in the camper. The bars are spring-loaded and are placed horizontally between the sides of the cabinet's doorframe to ensure nothing in the cabinet can come flying out. Inexpensive and easy to use, these bars are available in wood tones or chrome finishes.

PLATE STACKERS are a must-have if you prefer to eat off ceramic or porcelain plates, rather than the paper variety. These keep plates all in one place, safe and secure and chip free. You'll find plate stackers that can be screwed down inside cabinets, with rubberized sides that will nestle even delicate dinnerware. They come in assorted sizes and some are even adjustable.

KNIFE HOLDERS are as much a safety feature as a convenience. Not only do they keep knives from moving around, but they also prevent them from getting dull from collisions in a drawer. Make sure you buy a holder with a lock-in feature for travel, and one that is easy to clean—you want to avoid bacterial issues.

SLIDE-OUT DRAWERS are available for retrofitting under counters and under the dinette table. These are shallow containers that secure small items like decks of cards and silverware, while keeping them easy to get at.

DINETTES

Your camper's dinette can be awfully valuable real estate. Not only is it a place to eat a meal, but it's also an ideal workspace for travelers who need to get some business done during their vacation. The dinette is the natural center of family activity in the camper, a place where board games can be played in relative comfort. Some dinettes even fold down to provide extra sleeping space. But "comfort" is key to making any of those activities as pleasant and inviting as possible. Beat-up old cushions flattened to half their original thickness and a splintery, checkered, and wobbly dinette table are unpleasant features in any camper.

Updating a dinette table is a basic choice between reviving what's there and replacing it wholesale with one of the many options on the marketplace. You can also compromise, and add your own renovation, while buying a new table or cushions. Manufacturers offer each component separately, and you can find a suitable replacement—if not a direct match—for dinette elements in even vintage camper trailers.

But replacement is not the only solution. As long as the table itself and its support are not compromised, they can be revived. You can easily swap out edge banding or T-molding or trim around the edge of a dinette table, and that change alone may freshen up the look. Replace rusted edge banding by unscrewing it from around the table and cutting a replacement strip (available

THE APPLIANCE FACELIFT

So you spruced up all your cabinets with a coat of new paint and new hardware, and you've added a whole new dinette. Unfortunately, now your refrigerator and stove front are looking like the ugly cousins to everything else in your interior. Never fear, there's a much less expensive alternative to replacing appliances that are timeworn but otherwise working fine: paint them. You'll find appliance epoxy spray paint at large home centers and well-stocked hardware stores. Here's how easy the process is:

1 Thoroughly clean the appliance surface to be painted. Remove all grease, dirt, or residue.

2 Lightly sand the surface with a sanding sponge or 150-grit sandpaper.

3 Mask off any areas that might be hit with overspray.

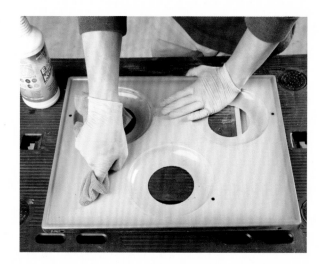

4 Use a smooth, even movement to spray on a light coat of the paint. Keep your hand moving and don't let any drips accumulate.

5 Wait 10 minutes, and then spray a second, light coat over the first. Let the appliance dry for 24 hours, remove the plastic and masking tape from the masked-off areas, and voilà—it looks like you've just bought new appliances.

through RV suppliers) and installing it with brand-new screws. To replace T-trim, tease up the edge of the trim with a utility knife or putty knife, and then use pliers to slowly and carefully pull out the old trim. Clean up the edge of any loose debris or old adhesive, then lay a thin bead of adhesive down and tap a new strip of T-trim into the edge channel with a rubber or wood mallet. Trim off the ends flush, and trim the edges with a new razor blade if you've used a wider trim than the original.

Trying to resurface a dinette table is rarely worth the effort. If the table's surface is so worn you want to replace it, a whole new table is probably the answer. Use a sheet of MDF or plywood, the same thickness as the existing table, as a blank to cut a new table. Use the old table as a template to trace a cutline on the MDF or plywood, and then cut out the shape with a jigsaw. Sand the edges and use a router with a thin edge-router bit to cut the channel for the T trim (unless you're using edge banding, in which case, predrill the holes for the banding). You can paint the surface with multiple layers of high-gloss enamel or use a sheet product such as Formica or veneer.

Ideally, a dinette table is sized to accommodate casual dining without feeling crowded. Keep in mind that the table is also a natural location for lounging or playing games on camping trips.

5

CAMPER MAINTENANCE AND TROUBLE-SHOOTING

If you go to all the trouble of bringing an older—or even a not-so-old—camper back to life, it only makes sense to keep it running as trouble-free and efficient as possible. Regular maintenance and a bit of preventive troubleshooting can head off more costly repairs down the line, and will ensure your camping trips are free of drama (and tow trucks).

Maintenance always precedes troubleshooting, so it comes first in this chapter. It's always wiser to take the time and effort to follow a regular schedule of maintenance than to put things off and wind up with a bigger problem on your hands—often when you're hundreds of miles from home or your trusted, local RV specialist.

MAINTENANCE

Decorating your camper is the fun and instantly rewarding part of owning one. You can pull up to a campsite and show off a bright new paint job, or revel in your ultra comfortable bed with the air conditioning blasting. But underneath all that enjoyment and fun is a solid maintenance schedule. Or, rather, maintenance schedules.

Different types of maintenance should be done at different times, but whether you're opening up your camper for the first trip of the season or just getting around to its once-yearly care routine, specific chores are meant to be done at specific times.

A WEIGHTY PROPOSITION

A frequent question among new camper owners is whether a trailer requires them to stop at highway weigh stations. For the vast majority of people, the answer is "no." Besides not being a commercial vehicle, most smaller (and most vintage) campers don't begin to approach the weight thresholds that would require stopping at a weigh station. The most common state-imposed limits on vehicle weight are 8,000, 10,000, and 26,000 pounds Gross Vehicle Weight (GVW). Those correspond to number of axles. However, in many states, rental moving trucks and vans and recreational vehicles—including both motorhomes

and travel trailers—are exempted from weigh stations. You should check with your local state's Department of Transportation or, if in doubt and pulling a large travel trailer, just pull into any open weigh station and they will likely wave you right through.

Regardless of when the maintenance is done, most of these practices require no special training or tools. They are just a matter of taking care of the small details so the larger details take care of themselves.

Aside from keeping your campsite beauty in good working order, basic maintenance is a wonderful way for new or first-time camper owners to become intimately familiar with their camper. Get to know it well enough and you'll develop a sixth sense for detecting problems before they occur and knowing just what the problem might be.

Before every trip, or any time you're traveling:

- **CHECK TIRE PRESSURE AND LUG NUT TIGHTNESS.** These two simple inspections will take less than two minutes, but they make for an easier towing experience and can also potentially prevent a catastrophic accident.

- **DISCONNECT HOOKUPS.** Whether you're using a shoreline at home or at a campground, make sure the power is disconnected and your shoreline stowed before driving away. Same goes for the potable water hookup. Not disconnecting hookups is one of the most common mistakes novice campers make at campgrounds.

- **CHANGE GENERATOR GAS.** Time slips away from us, and the time between camping trips can be a month or more. Strictly speaking, the shelf life of gasoline—under typical conditions—is only 30 days. If you're closing in on that since you last used the generator, a new batch of gas is a small price to pay to head off costly carburetor repair or replacement, or other generator malfunction and damage.

- **CHECK EXTERIOR LIGHTS AND BRAKES.** Before driving off on your first outdoor adventure of the season or heading home from a great vacation, enlist a helper to check that brake, backup, safety, and running lights are all operable and working properly. Also test that the trailer brakes are working correctly.

- **CHILL AND INSPECT THE REFRIGERATOR.** You'll want to begin cooling down the refrigerator at least 8 hours before you leave so that you can be sure it's cold by the time you reach the campground. Take the time to check the seal on the door, and replace as necessary.

- **TEST THAT ALARMS ARE IN GOOD WORKING ORDER.** Test your smoke alarm, carbon monoxide and oxygen sensor alarms, and any other air-quality or fire-prevention alarms. They should all be working properly before you spend your first night in the camper. Also check that your onboard fire extinguisher is fastened down and not expired.

Pre-chilling your refrigerator is one of those tasks that is easy to forget but can lead to a bad campsite stay and spoiled food.

- **SECURE OPENINGS.** Make sure all windows, vents, and access doors are securely fastened shut.

- **SHUT OFF WATER PUMP.** Make sure the water pump is off when moving a camper.

- **PRACTICE FIRE SAFETY.** Douse any campfire or outside cook fire. Make sure it's completely out before leaving the campsite.

Once you're home:

- **LEAVE VENTS OPEN AND WINDOWS CRACKED.** This will prevent overheating inside the camper.

- **CLEAN OUT WASTE.** Empty, flush, and clean the gray and black tanks unless you did that at the campsite. Depending on how long it will be until your next camping trip, you may want to empty your potable water supply and sanitize the system with a bleach flush.

- **PROTECT THE ROOF AND SKIN.** Ideally, cover your camper between camping trips. This may entail putting it in a garage, but more likely for most owners—and anyone who owns a larger travel trailer or fifth wheel—this means using a camper cover or tarp so that constant sun doesn't deteriorate the roof or dry out seals. If you use a cover, it should be breathable or there should be air circulation around the surface of the trailer.

Seasonally or yearly:

- **SERVICE THE GENERATOR.** Follow the manufacturer's recommendations, but it's usually a good idea to change the oil and filter in your generator twice a year.

- **INSPECT SEALS AND SEAMS.** This should be done twice a year and is a good habit to get into at the start and finish of the season. Start on the roof. Check seams closely and pay particular attention to the seals around roof fixtures like air vents and air-conditioning units. Next, check the seals around windows and doors, including access doors to exterior storage areas. Also check the seams under corner trim.

- **RECOAT A RUBBER ROOF.** Depending on the type of rubber roof you have, it's usually wise to recoat it once a year, at the start of the season (see page 78).

- **LUBRICATE SLIDE-OUT RAILS.** If you have a slide-out room or extension, lubricate the rails with a spray graphite lubricant at least twice a year.

- **SERVICE AIR-CONDITIONING.** Clean or replace air-conditioner filters.

- **INSPECT BRAKES.** Check your brake linings and the general state of the brake assembly once a year. This is a great chore to schedule right before the opening of the season. Take the opportunity to repack your wheel bearings (see page 82).

MAINTAIN TOWING INTEGRITY

Don't fall into the trap of just accepting how your vehicle tows a camper trailer. You can and should adjust tow hitch supports for a better, safer towing experience. For instance, a loss of traction can be due to excessive spring-bar tension, while light steering is the result of not enough spring-bar tension. If the hitch has excessive sway control, the tow vehicle steering will plow through corners; too little sway control translates to a trailer that sways easily and often. Excess trailer sway can also be caused by worn sway control friction surfaces or too little of the trailer weight load applied to the tongue (should be 12 to 15 percent of the total trailer weight). If you are hesitant to fiddle with your towing setup, you can have the local RV shop check it out and adjust for a minimal fee.

WINTERIZING A CAMPER

Depending on where you live, the winter months may be more or less brutal. In any case, if your camper is going to be sitting idle for a long period, you should carefully winterize it to ensure that no problems crop up during hibernation.

- **BATTERY ARRAY.** Remove 12-volt batteries from your camper and store them someplace well ventilated, warm, and dry. Freezing temperatures can destroy a battery, and remaining hooked up can slowly drain one. Clean the batteries before storing using a 1:1 mixture of baking soda and lukewarm water.

TIRE SHADE

Want to help your camper trailer tires last as long as possible and avoid any potential problems on the road? Tire covers are an easy and inexpensive preventive measure. Keep the tires under wraps at home and at the campsite, and you prevent deterioration from exposure to strong sunlight and rubber-destroying UV rays.

If you won't be using your camper in the colder months, it's important to properly winterize it—and even if you've taken precautions, leaving it outside all winter long is a recipe for extra problems.

- **TIRES.** Chock the wheels as a safety measure, even if you feel the storage area is relatively flat. If you're parking a trailer on grass or the bare ground, roll the tires on top of boards or other solid pads so that they don't freeze to the surface during freeze-thaw cycles. Inflate the tires to the maximum "cold" pressure recommended by the manufacturer.

- **LEVEL.** If the camper will be stored outside exposed to the elements, set it up slightly off-level (2 or 3 degrees) so that water and snow will be more likely to drain or slide off the roof.

- **PLUMBING.** A camper's plumbing is the system most likely to be adversely affected by storage in cold temperatures. There is a simple and important winterizing routine for any camper that contains a complete plumbing system.

1 Remove the potable water tank drain plug and allow the tank to drain completely.

2 Open all the taps, including indoor and outdoor showerheads, and allow them to drain completely.

3 Flush the toilet to drain any water from it.

4 Ensure that the water heater is turned off. Open the pressure-relief valve and remove the anode rod or other drain plug from the water heater. Allow the water heater to drain completely, and then replace the rod after wrapping the threads in Teflon tape. Close the pressure-relief valve.

5 If you haven't done so already, empty the black waste tank, and then the gray tank, and flush them both.

6 Close both the inlet and the outlet valves for the water heater.

7 Install a suction tube fitting in the freshwater tank line, if one hasn't been installed already. (The suction tube fitting is included in a winterizing kit, available at RV suppliers and larger hardware stores.)

8 Run the water pump for 15 seconds. Close all the taps.

9 Insert the suction tube into a container of RV antifreeze. *Caution: Use only RV antifreeze; it's nonpoisonous (unlike automotive antifreeze).* Turn on the water pump. Use the amount of antifreeze recommended by the camper's manufacturer, replacing antifreeze containers as they empty. Normally, the process uses 1 to 5 gallons of antifreeze, depending on the size of your camper and the capacity of your plumbing system. If you use too much, it will just be stored in the freshwater tank and won't do any harm.

ALTERNATIVE: With older campers, it can be difficult to access the line to install a suction tube fitting. Many owners of older, and especially vintage, campers simply pour the antifreeze directly into the freshwater tank fill port.

10 Turn on the water pump. Turn on the taps, one at a time, until the antifreeze begins to run out (both cold and hot taps). Repeat with the shower(s) and toilet. Close the taps and pour a small amount of antifreeze into each drain in the camper. Turn off the water pump. Clean up any spills.

- **LOCKS AND HINGES.** Lubricate all locks on the camper with graphite lubricant. Lubricate exposed screws and hardware, such as hitch locks, hitch handles, and screws on jacks, with spray-on silicone lubricant or white grease.

- **CONSUMABLES.** Remove any food, including condiments, spices, dry goods, and pet food. This is to prevent vermin infestation. For the same reason, place dryer fabric softener sheets around the trailer, in cabinets and drawers, in exterior storage areas, on and under mattresses, on the floor, and in other areas.

- **APPLIANCES.** Lock refrigerator doors open and unplug countertop appliances.

Just like the appliances in your home, a range and any other appliance in your camper will benefit from a regular thorough cleaning.

WINTER CAMPING

Are you a snow lover, someone who likes nothing better than parking your camper in a space smack in the middle of a deserted, high-country campsite in December?

That's understandable. Winter camping is an entirely different experience and can be a great alternative to expensive hotels for avid snowboarders or skiers. But using your camper in the coldest months requires some additional alterations to ensure you aren't left without water, heat, or other vital services. (Also keep in mind that many campgrounds close down for the winter.)

- **INSULATE TANKS AND EXPOSED PLUMBING.** Prevent disaster by insulating your freshwater supply, gray, and black holding tanks. Left unprotected, freezing temperatures could cause one or all of these to rupture. Some more modern travel trailers route excess heat from the furnace or interior of the camper down around the tanks to ensure they don't freeze (adding antifreeze to the waste tanks is another strategy that can be effective against freezing). This is an effective strategy as long as you have enough gas capacity to keep the furnace running even when the interior is heated. As an alternative to insulation, you can install electric heating tape similar to what homeowners use to prevent ice dams on roof edges and eaves. Or, if you spend most of your camping time in subzero temperatures, it probably makes sense to retrofit your unit with heated water storage and waste tanks. RV suppliers and marine plumbing outfitters offer heat tape and special heaters for exposed plumbing pipe.

- **PROTECT ANY WATER SUPPLY HOSE.** Cover the hose with an insulated sleeve—1-inch split foam pipe insulation can do the trick. You can also turn to heat tape to keep the pipe warm or, in a pinch, if the ground isn't frozen, dig a trench and cover the hose with soil.

- **STOP AIR LEAKS.** Check the weatherstripping around the entry door. This seal is usually too lightweight for cold weather. Consider replacing it with heavy-duty weatherstripping. For the same reason, make sure the door is a tight fit to the frame.

- **UPGRADE THE WINDOWS.** If you're an avid cold-weather camper, it will likely make good financial sense to swap your existing windows for insulated units. They cost a pretty penny but can return that cost in the long run over several seasons of near-freezing temperatures. Be aware that insulated camper windows can be a specialty item, and you may not find them in your window sizes. In that case, you may have to resort to window sealant film or similar treatments. You can even cut foil-backed insulation or insulation foam board to the size and shape of your windows, and use Velcro fasteners to secure them in place over the windows. These will help with cold nights when blocking the view won't matter.

- **BLOCK VENTS.** RV suppliers offer a selection of vent "cushions" that can be used to block hot air from rising and escaping out of air-conditioning and other rooftop vents.

BASIC TROUBLESHOOTING

The big nightmare for most camper trailer owners is to be far away from civilization, perhaps even boondocking in a remote location, and suddenly have a problem with the camper. In some cases, it may even happen far out of cell phone range. No matter what, the first line of defense is to not panic and to avoid making the problem worse. That usually means not attempting to remedy a situation until you get home. However, there are some stopgap measures you can take to get through any problem.

- **SYSTEMS.** The good news is that most of a camper's systems don't actually affect how the trailer moves. That means that you can wait until you get home or to an RV shop before actually repairing the system. In general, unless you feel confident that you can remedy a systems problem, it's best to shut down the system and not use fixtures until you get back home. This may entail not showering and using an external bathroom, going without air conditioning or heat, or not using any powered appliances. The key point is that you don't want to make a problem worse for the foolish reason of jumping in on a repair without having the proper tools or facilities on hand. In a worst-case scenario, you can always cut your vacation short and head home.

- **EXTERIOR SURFACES.** Some of the most common damage to a camper trailer occurs at campgrounds: collision with natural obstacles navigating—and especially backing up—on dicey campground roads and slips. All it takes is a low-hanging branch or a sharp rock to do damage that requires your immediate attention. The secret is to come prepared by packing a few emergency supplies that will serve you well no matter what the accidental damage.

Tires are some of the most vulnerable parts of a trailer. Obviously, it's wise to keep a spare. But if you don't, you should definitely store a couple of cans of aerosol tire inflator-sealer. This product is sprayed right into the valve of a flat tire. It contains an expanding foam that seals punctures while the air in the can fills the tire. The seal won't last forever, but it will last long enough for you to make your way to a repair shop.

Roofs and siding are also extremely vulnerable to campground damage. That's why you should keep "RV roof patch" in your storage compartment at all times. This tape is a quick solution to punctures or tears in camper roof surfaces. Buy roof patch meant for the material your roof is made of, and if different, a different patch for your siding. In either case, you simply clean the damaged area and apply the tape right over it. That will keep any water and bugs out in the short term. But, like the tire inflating spray, it's not a long-term solution. Fix the damage at the first opportunity after your return home from your trip.

THE GREAT BIG CAMPER TRAILER TROUBLESHOOTING GUIDE

FURNACE

Problem	Solution
Pilot light won't light or won't stay lit	Start with the gas supply: the canister may be empty; adjust the gas pressure to the correct setting; check tank regulator—bad regulator may be shutting down flow of gas; check and adjust the spark gap; clean the pilot orifice; purge the gas line of any air and adjust the pilot screw; check the thermocouple for failure
Fan doesn't come on, no heat	Check power from battery; check circuit breaker/fuse; check thermostat by removing cover and inspecting anticipator wire; set temperature to maximum and slide adjuster until fan comes on; if still no fan, replace thermostat
Burner will not light	Turn on or reset thermostat; make sure gas supply is on and tank is full; adjust gas pressure; ensure battery is charged; clean sail switch and replace if defective; check wiring and duct hoses for defects; check for blocked air intake or burner exhaust; check electrode lead is sparking igniter and adjust spark gap; clean connections and clean or replace jet
Fan but no heat	Low airflow from the blower; check power to blower motor—may be drained battery or wiring problem such as a short; weak airflow can be due to blockage; check registers to ensure they are not closed; test the regulator valve is functioning properly with a manometer; check electronic furnace ignition contacts are properly spaced—not too far apart or touching
Blower doesn't run	Check voltage at furnace; check fuse and wire connections; check that thermostat points are closing; rotate the motor to ensure it hasn't locked up; test relay and replace if not working; replace motor

REFRIGERATOR

Problem	Solution
Not getting cold enough	Check and adjust thermostat; ensure air circulation around refrigerator; level refrigerator/trailer; check for door gasket failure and replace if necessary; check connections and that heater is getting correct voltage; check fuse or breaker; replace defective thermostat or cooling unit
Overcooling	Check thermostat for correct setting; check thermostat lead placement in refrigerator; replace defective thermostat; check wiring in heater

ROOF AIR CONDITIONER

Problem	Solution
A/C doesn't run	Check connection to power source; check breaker or fuse; test switch with multimeter and replace if defective
Fan runs slowly	Check electrical connections; check voltage at unit (may be too low); check alignment of the blower fan; clean or replace filters
Fan runs but compressor does not come on	Check that compressor is getting power; change to correct size power cord; check capacitor for failure; reset thermostat or replace if defective; check time delay switch and replace if not working
Compressor doesn't shut off	Thermostat set too low; clean condenser and coils; if evaporator is iced, let thaw; replace a thermostat stuck on setting; if refrigerant leak or undercharged, fix leak and recharge

FRESHWATER SUPPLY

Problem	Solution
Foul odor or bad taste	Mix 1 cup bleach with 1 cup cold water, add to tank, and fill tank; run faucets until bleach smell is apparent; let sit for 24 hours before flushing system
Tank leaks	Check hoses for loose connection; inspect tank for cracks or freeze damage
Tank won't fill	Clear vent hose clog
Water pump runs but no water	Low water level in tank; check water line for clogs, kinks, or binds; check for leak in suction line; tighten clamps on suction line; check pump for punctured diaphragm, cracked housing, broken pump belt, stuck backflow valve, or worn impeller; clean in-line filter
Water pump cycles on and off with faucets closed	Inspect plumbing for water leak in lines or faucets; check for defective toilet valve; check pump for internal leak or failed pressure switch
Water pump won't run	Check that master switch is on and check fuse or breaker; charge low battery; check that wiring connections are secure; replace defective pump motor
Water pump stays on when faucets are closed	Check water tank level; charge batteries; repair leaking faucets; check pressure switch and replace if failed
Low water flow	Check pump suction line for leak; check for kinked outlet line and clogged intake strainer; check for leak in pump diaphragm
Sputtering water flow	Check suction line for leak; bleed air from lines; bleed hot-water lines

WATER HEATER/HOT WATER SUPPLY

Problem	Solution
Pilot goes out	Clean or replace orifice; check thermocouple for failure; check and adjust gas pressure; clean air intake tube and adjust air shutter

Pilot goes out when lighting flame	Wait 1 minute for thermocouple to heat; tighten thermocouple connection; replace failed thermocouple; replace gas control
No spark in direct ignition heater	Adjust spark gap; clean terminals; replace electrodes; replace lead wire; clean system
Early lockout	Check for reverse polarity and reverse ground and power wires if necessary; reestablish ground connection; check gas pressure and lower if necessary; adjust the sensor probe position in the flame
Unstable burner flame	Check orifice for blockage and clean; realign burner tube and remove any obstruction in the burner; adjust the air shutter and check and adjust gas pressure; refill gas tank
Yellow flame	Adjust the air shutter; clean the orifice and burner tube; adjust gas pressure; clear grill; realign burner jet
Excess smoke or soot	Adjust air shutter; clear and realign burner jet; refill low gas supply
Burner won't light	Check, clear, and adjust burner jet; adjust air shutter; clear tube obstruction; set thermostat higher or lower; replace malfunctioning gas control valve
Relief valve leakage	Flip valve handle to clear any blockage; purge air in system; replace bad valve

BATTERY/BATTERY BANK

Problem	Solution
Batteries use excessive water; visible cap deposits; warpage; other deformations	Possibly overcharging: check for malfunctioning regulator or converter; if deformed, replace the battery
Battery won't hold charge	Check that the battery is secure and not vibrating, that the terminal connections are tight; test regulator and converter; tighten the fan belt and perform a trickle charge; replace the battery if it still won't charge
Appliances won't run on 12V power	Recharge the batteries and perform a load test; check water; tighten the terminals and clean off any corrosion; check for loose wiring; check fuses

ONBOARD AIR CONDITIONER

Problem	Solution
Unit doesn't come on	Check fuse or breaker; check power source or inverter; test switch with multimeter
Fan blows slow/weak	Check electrical connections; check that power cord or extension cord is correct size; clean or replace air filters
Compressor does not come on even when fan is blowing	Check power output (voltage may be too low); check for correct power cord size; check thermostat setting (may be too low); have professional check for defective thermostat, capacitor, or compressor
Compressor does not shut off	Set the thermostat higher; clean the condenser; contact technician to check switch and possibly recharge refrigerant

LP GAS SYSTEM

Problem	Solution
Regulator frozen	This can be due to an overfilled tank or clogged regulator vent; clean the vent and, if the problem persists, contact a certified technician
Pilot light failure	Check that the regulator output pressure is not too low; make sure the gas cylinder is not nearly empty; check thermocouple for defect; clean regulator vent

FLUORESCENT LIGHTS

Problem	Solution
Won't light	Polarity reversed in fixture, rewire black/positive and white/negative; tube failure

Tube ends blackened	Limit on-offs; check and recharge battery and inspect connections (low voltage); tube failure
Repetitive ballast failure	Bad tubes—replace; check and recharge battery and inspect connections (low voltage); have power converter tested for voltage spikes

GENERATOR

Problem	Solution
Won't start	Check battery and charge or replace; check fuel level; clean terminals and check battery cables; replace air filter; clean and adjust or replace ignition points; replace malfunctioning coil; clean and adjust carb choke; check starter fuse
Difficult to start	Replace fuel (stale); adjust carb and point gap; replace air cleaner and spark plug; replace faulty fuel pump
Engine stops unexpectedly	Check fuel level and oil pressure/level; adjust fuel mixture; clean or replace spark plug and fuel filter; replace solenoid
Black smoke	Adjust carb; replace air filter; clean and adjust choke
Engine surge	Clean or replace air filter; replace ignition points and plug; check and clean or replace fuel filter and pump; adjust carb; replace fuel with fresh; clean and lubricate linkage
Overheating	Clean air inlet and outlet; adjust carb mixture (too lean); adjust points
No current from generator	Check breaker or fuse; check wiring for short; have generator professionally serviced

TRAILER BRAKES (ELECTRIC)

Problem	Solution
Brakes not effective	Check connections from tow vehicle; check that trailer is properly grounded; check brake drum magnets and replace if weak or not working; adjust brakes; check for corrupted or worn pad linings and out-of-round drums; use separate circuit for lights; reduce oversized load
Brakes don't work	Check connections and wiring for break or loose connection; check wiring diagram for correct wiring; adjust brakes; check magnets; inspect connector plug for contaminants; check resistor continuity and replace if necessary
Brake surge	Turn or replace out-of-round drums; check that the trailer is properly grounded; check magnets; check bearings and replace and/or repack
Brake noise	Check pad linings and brake springs and replace any that are overly or unusually worn; check bearings and replace and/or repack; adjust brakes; adjust star wheel adjuster until there is strong drag and then back off slightly; check for uneven wear; check magnets in need of possible replacement
Brakes grab or lock	Check that axle flanges are correctly installed; inspect pad linings for grease or other debris; adjust brake system controller; inspect springs for breaks or damage and replace if necessary
Brakes drag	Check that brakes are properly adjusted; replace hydraulic controller pins and coil; check that flanges are properly installed; inspect brake assembly for corrosion; check if springs are worn, broken, or damaged

TRAILER HITCHES

Problem	Solution
Coupler comes off ball	Inspect the ball clamp for damage or failure (it may have been a one-time error in properly securing the clamp when hitching up); confirm that the ball is the appropriate size for the coupler and replace if necessary

Spring bar falls out	Check the retaining clips for failure, or they may be missing; improper installation
Unusual hitch noise	Lubricate the ball; tighten the bolts connecting receiver structure to tow vehicle; lubricate ends of spring bars
Tow vehicle handling affected	Unhitch trailer and carefully rehitch following manufacturer's recommended procedure; check that ball height is correct and adjust as necessary; check and set ball angle to keep spring bars level and keep at least four chain links under tension

TRAILER TIRES

Problem	Solution
Wear bars apparent	Replace the tires immediately (both sides)
Inside edge/outside edge wear	Camber off, have professional align tires; worn suspension members, have professional check the suspension; outside edge wear may be caused by low tire pressure, check tire pressure before every trip
Center wear	Tires overinflate, adjust to correct tire pressure
Cupping (also called scalloping) on tread	Can be caused by excess wear of any suspension member, including shocks, A-arm, or bushings and ball joints; check tire for round and replace rim if necessary; balance tires; inspect both brakes and bearings for defects
Bulging or bubble in sidewall	Replace tires immediately
Squealing	Check tire pressure for underinflation; have alignment of tires checked; ensure the tires are rated for the load
Slow leak	Check treads for puncture debris; smear cooking oil around valve stem to detect stem leak; check rim for damage or defect and replace if necessary

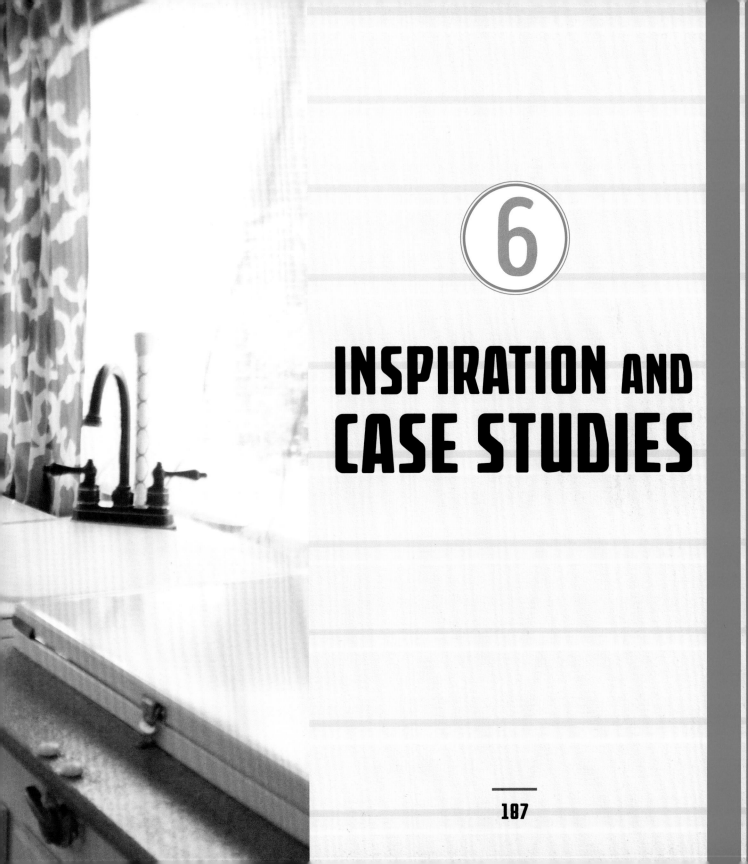

6

INSPIRATION AND CASE STUDIES

Before you create your own signature camper trailer design, it can be helpful to see how others approach the challenge. That's what this chapter is here for. The case studies that follow feature radically different living quarters done in up in radically different ways. The common denominators are that all the designers had to deal with space constraints and functional concerns such as crafting a stunning interior that was still leak-proof and easy to clean. Use these walkthroughs as pure inspiration to build on in your own rolling palace, or steal ideas and make them your own (we won't tell).

AIRSTREAMING LIVING QUARTERS

Andreas Stavropoulos wasn't your average outdoor adventurer looking for a vacation camper. The co-founder of Base Landscape in San Francisco was looking for living quarters, an interesting room he could park outside the local co-op housing where he was a member. The idea was to have spacious live-work quarters, with the main co-op house as a place to cook and bathe. He found the ideal lodgings abandoned in the middle of a Salinas property overgrown with weeds. For the tidy sum of $4,600, he was the proud new owner of a mistreated 1959 Airstream travel trailer.

To say the trailer had seen better days was an understatement. The neglected camper had, at one time, been home to a vagrant as well as a population of mice. The interior aluminum cladding had been covered front to back in flesh-toned paint. There was rot in the floor. Andreas had his work cut out for him.

The first challenge was to find a space where he could park the trailer and have room to work on it. Fortunately, he had a sculptor friend who was working on an MFA at Stanford, and offered a large barn-studio space.

Andreas Stavropoulos outside the 1959 Airstream he renovated into garden living quarters. *Andreas Stavropoulos*

ABOVE: Stavropoulos made the most of the interior aluminum surface by stripping each end of the trailer's interior walls. Not only is it a cool look, but the metal surfaces also reflect light, keeping the interior bright and cheery throughout the day. *Andreas Stavropoulos*

LEFT: The workspace section of the trailer not only includes a view, but the cork flooring also provides a warm surface underfoot. *Andreas Stavropoulos*

Andreas essentially gutted the interior because so little was worth keeping. He replaced the rotted sections of the subfloor, stripped the interior end caps back to the original aluminum, and painted the rest of the interior a calming light green.

Along the way, he discovered that the trailer was one of the last years Airstream used a "dual-wall" system, with aluminum cladding as both the exterior skin and the interior wall surface (the expense of using so much aluminum eventually forced the company to move to vinyl interior surfaces).

To keep as much of the interior height as possible, Andreas used thin cork flooring. It added an informal, natural look and was warm underfoot on chilly Bay Area mornings. He built new cabinetry from birch plywood that perfectly complemented the light and airy look Andreas had already established in the interior. The look was, not coincidentally, sleek, modern, and upscale. That wasn't an accident.

As Andreas recounts, "I think one of the reasons I was attracted to a project like that, and why a lot of people are attracted to smaller projects, is that you can use nicer materials. The area you're covering is so significantly less than the average sprawling house that you can afford to splurge on flooring or other elements."

The custom cabinetry is simply constructed of birch plywood with hole-saw holes for handles. The aftermarket lighting fixtures were easy to tie into the trailers existing wiring, one of the few features on the trailer that wasn't degraded beyond use. *Andreas Stavropoulos*

A queen mattress and down comforter make the sleeping quarters a draw day or night. *Andreas Stavropoulos*

Restoring the exterior to original was a no-brainer because the Airstream's distinctive exterior surface is so much a part of the trailer's charm. The polishing process, however, was far from the most enjoyable part of the project for Andreas. "If I had to do it again, I would definitely hire somebody . . . ideally someone who polishes boats." Although not technically challenging, polishing an entire Airstream exterior takes an inordinate amount of time and elbow grease (see for yourself on page 75).

The effort Andreas put into the project speaks for itself. After adapting the electrical system to AC so that it could be plugged into the main house, the trailer became a cozy, efficient living space. Andreas recently sold the trailer to friends who will also use it as living quarters, extending the new life of this old classic.

A COOL COLEMAN

Ramie Babcock traces her fondness for campers to her grandparents' 1978 Scamper. After camping trips, her grandmother would clean the camper top to bottom and leave it in the driveway to air out, windows and door wide open. The camper was an invitation to Ramie and her cousins, and they spent many happy hours playing in their own driveway castle. She was even more

Before the remodel, the pop-up camper was clean and damage free, if a bit ho-hum with predictable wood veneer surfaces, brown curtains, and a forgettable brown vinyl floor. The blue tablecloth and bedding were the early, Band-Aid solutions to spruce up the design. *Courtesy of Ramie Babcock*

intrigued later, when her grandmother revitalized the interior with new handmade drapes and upholstery, giving the home on wheels its own unique look.

Fast-forward to one lazy Saturday when adult Ramie was glancing through Craigslist garage sale posts, only to find an enticing ad for a pristine 2000 Coleman pop-up. Despite her husband's hesitance to launch into a new family project, Ramie plunked down $2,000 from a rainy-day fund and became the proud new owner of her very own pop-up gem.

The camper was in remarkably good shape—no leaks, broken fixtures, or obvious structural damage. It was good to go. It even had a bathroom (the lack of one would be a deal-breaker for Ramie, who is not a fan of tent camping for just that reason).

As nice as the camper was, it was bland. Ramie wanted to make it a home away from home and put her own signature on the interior. She focused her efforts on three "big-bang-for-the-buck" changes: upholstery, flooring, and countertops. The adventure started with a visit to a local crafts store. "I went about it like a Pinterest board. I grabbed a bunch of fabric swatches and laid them out right in the middle of the store's floor. I wanted to see how different colors and fabrics would work together. I knew we wanted calming colors and

TOP: The bolt of mix-and-match fabrics Ramie Babcock used for her camper rehab, laid out on the floor of the store—a great way to make sure colors and patterns will work together. *Courtesy of Ramie Babcock*

BOTTOM: Want to stay on top of a camper rehab? Follow Ramie's lead and make a detailed list of what needs to be done in what order. It may seem a bit obsessive, but it's the only way to make sure things don't fall through the cracks and you don't wind up making multiple trips to the hardware store when one would have sufficed. *Courtesy of Ramie Babcock*

TOP: The cabinets in the Coleman pop-up were rot free and structurally sound, so updating them just meant removing doors and tops, priming, and painting them a space-opening lighter color. *Courtesy of Ramie Babcock*

BOTTOM: The base walls were primed and painted at the same time as the cabinets, making for an economy of scale in effort and paint supplies. *Courtesy of Ramie Babcock*

LEFT: The vinyl-plank "wood" floors were easy to install. They are simply cut to fit and snapped together. The look is super-realistic and the price is well within even the most modest rehab budget. *Courtesy of Ramie Babcock*

RIGHT: The cabinets continue to look brand-new thanks to a couple of coats of sturdy, glossy white enamel. The vinyl floor provides the perfect backdrop for the cabinets, creating a stunning look. *Courtesy of Ramie Babcock*

geometric shapes, and from there it was just fun. That was the most fun of anything in the whole project, just picking out all of the colors and patterns and seeing how they worked together."

Reupholstering the dinette cushions was less fun and the biggest challenge because it involved a steep learning curve. As Ramie admits, "My family sews. I'm the only one who doesn't. So the actual sewing part, which should have taken three days, took a week. It was a lot of trial and error, and loads of questions at the fabric store."

Ramie wanted the same look for the floors in her camper that she had for the floors in her house, so she picked a wood-patterned vinyl plank floor that was easy to install and went in right over the existing vinyl sheet flooring.

The cabinet at the corner of the bed opposite the sink is actually the bench top covering the onboard toilet; the curtain behind pulls out to form a privacy screen (right). *Courtesy of Ramie Babcock*

She also decided to upgrade the camper's countertops with a Rust-Oleum Countertop Transformations kit. The kit includes all the material necessary to create a new countertop appearance by embedding vinyl flakes in an epoxy resin over the existing surface. Ramie's two sons had a blast helping in the project, and the camper renovation became a family affair.

The transformation turned a modest pop-up into a super-comfy camper that includes an indoor and outdoor shower (stock), an onboard cartridge toilet, and a cooktop that detaches and can be mounted on a support on the outside of the camper for great outdoor meals (and no smell inside). Ramie maintains a strict no-shoes policy and has organized the inside so that even given the small footprint, there's a place for everything that might go along on any given trip.

That's not much, because Ramie and her husband decided early on that they wouldn't bring any electronics along with them. Theirs is a pure camping experience, where they enjoy the simple comforts of a clean, tidy, pretty pop-up. Ramie's two-wheeled getaway has just enough space for her family of four to relax when they're not taking nature hikes and to play board games when the inevitable downpour strikes. Whatever the case, it's all done in simple, gracious style.

The finished camper features a calming color scheme of greens and browns, and includes refaced countertops and dinette, a dirt-hiding and easy-to-clean floor, and visually interesting patterns. *Courtesy of Ramie Babcock*

ROLLING ARCHITECTURE

In 2011, Matthew Hofmann founded Hofmann Architecture (also called HofArc) as a wholly different type of architecture firm. Not content to simply design traditional buildings, he opted to create rolling pieces of art from vintage campers. The family-run business—his father, Wally, is the general manager of the firm—has built its reputation on a unique and luxurious minimalist design style, a celebration of small space living, and a reinterpretation of what classic travel trailers and campers can become when you combine refined craftsmanship with classic and iconic elements.

Matthew Hofmann (left) and father Wally. *Hofmann Architecture*

HofArc's creations seamlessly mix modern and vintage. Although the firm's portfolio includes all types of vessels, it is best known for its work on classic aircraft aluminum trailers, such as Airstreams and Spartans. HofArc rehabs the exterior of these trailers to the original stunning mid-century (or earlier) appearance, while reinventing the interiors. The designs are inspired and fresh and often incorporate interesting original components that add style and authenticity.

Thirty-four-year-old Matthew worked out his design style and travel trailer–crafting chops on a 1978 27-foot Airstream Trade Wind that he aptly titled "Visionary." It served as his living quarters while he experimented with how to include features that were at once elegant, useful, and space conserving. That first camper showcased Matthew's design sensibility, which is simplicity itself. The trailer featured wood floors and countertops, a spare white-and-gray color scheme, a remarkably comfortable bathroom with vessel sink, and tasteful accents like a mosaic backsplash in the colors of the ocean.

Since that first Airstream, the firm has designed more than 300 unique creations, each one defined by the client's dreams and goals. Each is also marked by original designs, guided by Matthew's vision. As elegant and sophisticated as the looks are, the visual appeal is rivaled by the spectacular craftsmanship that goes into each camper.

That craftsmanship is as much simple hard work as it is figuring out the fine details that go into laying mosaic tile in a trailer, or bringing aluminum skin back to mirrored brilliance. Shockingly, the company doesn't keep those techniques a secret. Matthew has filmed a series of YouTube videos describing how to do just about everything the firm does to a trailer. Viewers will have to supply their own elbow grease and attention to detail.

But more and more, the firm is training and using subcontractors from across the United States to execute their designs, leaving the Hofmanns and HofArc's staff to focus on new directions and new ideas. Among the most dynamic of those is AXÍA, a completely new trailer company that HofArc is launching. AXÍA will redefine what a travel trailer can be. The super-light trailer will be built to last "for generations," in a modular format adaptable to the individual owner's preferences. It will include state-of-the-art materials and space-efficient layouts, with luxury options available. It is the natural extension of HofArc's portfolio, a bold new experiment that builds on the best from what the firm has already done.

"ELF": 1970 27-FOOT AIRSTREAM OVERLAND

HofArc describes this as a playful, uncomplicated space. It's an apt description. Built for a Santa Barbara ranch owner, the Elf is an intimate retreat for the owners and a guesthouse for visitors. The trailer was designed to be easily adaptable, serving different purposes at different times. The functional and comfortable "studio" space features bamboo flooring throughout the main area as well as interior walls that have been covered in simple, bright white, environmentally friendly zero-VOC paint. The trailer also boasts state-of-the-art systems, with hard-plumbed freshwater and waste systems and a built-in hutch for the 12-volt and 25-amp service panel. The bathroom includes a residential, full-height toilet, river rock flooring, miniature subway tiles on the walls, and a glass shower wall, creating a stall with a sleek linear drain.

A few portable furnishings allow for an instantaneous facelift to the blank canvas of the trailer's interior. *Hofmann Architecture*

The Elf's main space doesn't hurt for natural light. The white walls add to the sense of spaciousness in what is, in reality, a small room.
Hofmann Architecture

RIGHT: The full-service bathroom hides behind a wood-framed bathroom door with a "whole milk" Plexiglas insert.
Hofmann Architecture

BELOW: The luxurious bathroom features a frameless glass shower divider and a porcelain, vanity-top sink.
Hofmann Architecture

"HOLLY": 1969 26-FOOT AIRSTREAM OVERLANDER

This modest trailer offers two separate semiprivate sleeping spaces, allowing it to accommodate a family of four or two couples. HofArc kept the original floor plan, adding luxury touches, such as a bamboo dinette table, hardwood flooring, and new appliances. Blue glass tiles add a splash of color to the bathroom floor and walls, and two brand-new skylights bring in a wealth of natural light and are fitted with roller shades for when things get too bright and warm. Holly is an example of how Matthew integrates modern appliances and systems into a vintage structure. The trailer includes a commercial sink faucet, a thermostatically controlled propane furnace, and a complete solar system with battery array, panels, and inverter.

This trailer was honored by the American Institute of Architects (AIA) at the organization's 2013 convention in Denver, Colorado, where Matthew and Wally spent a weekend showing off its graces to attendees.

Holly's bathroom sparkles with simplicity and a functional layout that fits a sink and counter, toilet, and stand-up shower in a very small footprint. *Hofmann Architecture*

ABOVE: The red cushions on the bench seat and dinette provide a bit of bold relief from the otherwise black-and-white interior. *Hofmann Architecture*

LEFT: The contemporary kitchen offers abundant and secure cabinet space with a durable Corian counter and professional-quality cooktop. The look is super clean and easy to keep organized. *Hofmann Architecture*

The view from the spacious dining area. The fresh and fun striped awning outside offers much-needed shade during the hottest part of the day. The sink side of the kitchen includes a dishwasher and deep sink. *Hofmann Architecture*

"LUCKY": 1985 31-FOOT AIRSTREAM EXCELLA

Matthew personally designed this Airstream to capture the spirit of wanderlust that so embodied the trailers in their heyday. Although marked by his signature streamlined aesthetic, it features splashes of luxury and eye-catching design elements that are also practical and durable. No space is wasted in this elegant reimagining.

The idea behind the rehab was to divide the slightly longer-than-average trailer's space into clearly defined living and sleeping areas. That this trailer could just as easily be used as long-term living quarters as it could lodging on a camping trip is reinforced by the incredibly comfortable bedroom and amenities, such as the onboard clothes washer/dryer combo.

Lucky features a number of beautiful highlights, including reclaimed wood cabinet facing, Corian countertops, bamboo flooring (except in the bathroom, where it's teak!), and a solar panel system.

The bathroom in this travel trailer surrenders no comfort to space, with a shining, stylish vessel sink and modern faucet, and a stand-up shower with a paddle wand showerhead that makes showering comfortable regardless of the occupant's height. *Hofmann Architecture*

Among the most engaging elements in this trailer is the reclaimed-wood cabinet facing, a design feature that adds warmth and a natural appeal to an otherwise starkly modern space. *Hofmann Architecture*

RIGHT: The combo clothes washer and dryer adds a unique element to this trailer, one that makes it even more appropriate as long-term or even permanent housing. *Hofmann Architecture*

BELOW: Lucky's bedroom is a dream-inducing space with an 8" memory foam mattress, a ceiling vent, and a delicious cross breeze courtesy of operable windows on three sides of the room. *Hofmann Architecture*

The Playa's dining area encourages lingering, with a spacious wraparound banquette, a butcher block table, and light-blocking custom shades that keep the area cool during the hottest part of the day. *Hofmann Architecture*

"PLAYA": 1979 31-FOOT AIRSTREAM SOVEREIGN

The Spanish word for "beach," Playa was designed as a vacation getaway capturing the fun and relaxing nature of time spent soaking up the sun, some music, and not much else. It's a low-maintenance, easygoing travel trailer that is a breeze to clean after a long weekend of surf and sand.

A full-height refrigerator and abundant storage foster a relaxing vibe by allowing for the owners to bring all their favorite food and drink—and everything they might need to prepare those—without cramming anything in. A swivel-arm-mounted TV provides many viewing angles, and the generator comes on automatically when the battery array is low. A high-end Bose sound system puts the icing on the cake, in a trailer designed for maximum relaxation and recreation.

ABOVE: The bedroom encourages staying in bed, with a wealth of bedside surfaces to store whatever you might need for relaxation. A headboard shelf complements the large bedside table, and a flexible-neck modern reading light allows one person to finish a book while the other partner sleeps. *Hofmann Architecture*

LEFT: The wet room includes a teak wood floor and white penny tile, with a high-end shower column and showerhead—all the better to clean the sand off quickly and easily after a day at the beach. The bathroom also includes a high-profile residential toilet. *Hofmann Architecture*

Gourmet meals are a breeze to create in this kitchen outfitted with a four-burner, chef-quality cooktop. Cleanup is just as easy, with a deep undermount sink and restaurant-worthy faucet. *Hofmann Architecture*

RESOURCES

Airstream Supply
www.airstreamsupply.com
(801) 972-2400

If you're the owner of an iconic Airstream trailer, you'll find a wealth of specific replacement parts—as well as gifts, accessories, and more—on this eclectic website.

Bradd and Hall
www.braddandhall.com
(800) 445-1830

Sit in comfort with RV furnishings from Bradd and Hall. The company produces replace and retrofit sofas, dinette tables, cabinets, and more—from the sturdy and simple, to the ultra-luxurious.

Camco
www.camco.net
(800) 334-2004

Discover a complete line of small parts for your camper, hoses for every type of RV use, cleaners, fittings, filters, and more at Camco.

Camping World
www.campingworld.com
(888) 626-7576

If you can put it on, into, or over a camper, chances are that you'll find it at Camping World. As a one-stop-shop representing many different manufacturers, this resource makes finding what you need easy.

CH Camper Company
www.chcamper.com
(423) 802-9804

Want a sparkling vintage camper but can't spare the time to restore one? Turn to CH Camper Company, a manufacturer producing replicas of iconic CH "canned ham" trailers. They also offer replacement parts if yours needs a little updating.

Dometic

www.dometic.com

Need a new refrigerator for that Airstream? Or maybe you have to replace your camper's microwave. Whatever the appliance, you'll probably find it at Dometic—from air conditioners, to water heaters, cooktops, and beyond.

Girard Systems

www.girardrv.com

(800) 382-8442

Girard offers a wide selection of retractable awnings for RVs.

Happier Camper

www.happiercamper.com

(470) 222-6728

The Happier Camper produces an ultra-lightweight, retro-style tiny camper that is easy to tow, with a modular design that can be customized to the user. You won't find a bathroom or full kitchen inside, but it is a big step up from sleeping in a tent and super-cool to boot.

Motion Windows

www.rvwindows.com

(360) 944-4446

This company provides stock replacement and custom windows in single- or double-pane construction, with a wide assortment of tints and frame colors.

National Serro Scotty Organization

www.nationalserroscotty.org

If you're a fan of these charming little travel trailers you can join like-minded campers, swap resources, and learn more about the Serro Scotty on the website for this nationwide group.

On the Go

www.portablewatersoftener.com

(866) 482-9614

Beat the hard water blues with one of this company's portable water softeners that can be plumbed right into your trailer's fresh water system.

RV Parts Nation

www.rvpartsnation.com

(574) 264-5575

A one-stop retailer supply nose-to-tail camper equipment and supplies, including appliances, hardware, and interior and exterior kits for rehabbing different areas of a camper.

Vintage Campers

www.vintagecampers.com

(765) 473-8088

If you're going to keep your older camper trailer on the road, you're probably going to need some older parts. You can probably find what you need here.

Vintage Trailer Crazy

www.vintagetrailercrazy.com

(949) 689-3964

Prefer not to do your own camper rehab? Never fear, you can find a pre-rehabbed camper on this camper classifieds site that includes a full range of older beauties.

Vintage Trailer Supply

www.vintagetrailersupply.com

(800) 644-4620

With an amazing inventory of small and large replacement parts, and a complete section dedicated to how-to information, Vintage Trailer Supply is a one-stop-shop for trailer restorations and glamper hopefuls everywhere.

Winegard

www.winegard.com

Suppliers of RV antennas for broadband, Wi-Fi, TV, and other uses.

PHOTO CREDITS

Illustrations by Jeremy Kramer. Photography by Rich Fleischman, with assistance by Georgiy Vyrlan and Denis Vyrlan, except the following:

Cover and frontis: Shutterstock, shtiel; Page 4: Shutterstock, Aleksey Stemmer; page 6: Shutterstock, Chippix; page 7: Airstream Inc.; page 8: CH Camper Company; page 9: Shutterstock, Oksana Perkins; page 10: Shutterstock, Joseph Sohm; page 11: Shutterstock, Joseph Sohm; page 12: Shutterstock, Reinhard Tiburzy; page 13: Shutterstock, Teri Virbickis; page 14: Shutterstock, Phillip Lange; page 15: Shutterstock, Andy Dean Photography; page 16: Shutterstock, Kent Weakley; page 18: Airstream, Inc; page 19: Capri Camper; page 22: Shutterstock, Joseph Sohm; page 23: Shutterstock, oksana.perkins; page 24: Shutterstock, defotoberg; page 26: Shutterstock, Arina P Habich; page 27: Shutterstock, ABC Photo; page 31: Shutterstock, HildaWeges Photography; page 32: CH Camper Company; page 33: Shutterstock, Joshua Rainey Photography; page 39: CURT Manufacturing; page 40: CURT Manufacturing; page 42: Shutterstock, Philip Lange; page 44: Thetford; page 45: Thetford; page 48 left: Shutterstock, ABC Photo; page 48 right: Shutterstock, Baloncici; page 49: Thetford; page 50: Shutterstock, Arina P Habich; page 52: Shutterstock, Baloncici; page 53: Shutterstock, Joseph Sohm; page 59: Shutterstock, Arina P Habich; page 62: CH Camper Company; page 63: Dub-Box-USA.com; page 66: Shutterstock, Oksana.Perkins; page 68: Thetford; page 74: Shutterstock, Joseph Sohm; page 75: Shutterstock, klom; page 87: CURT Manufacturing; page 98: Shutterstock, Joseph Sohm; page 100: Shutterstock, Arina P Habich; page 102 bottom: mihalec; page 103 top: Shutterstock, Vereshchagin Dmitry; page 103 bottom: Shutterstock, Paul Vasarhelyi; page 105: Alamy Stock Photo, Tomasz Zajda; page 109: Alamy Stock Photo, Jim Parkin; page 110: Shutterstock, Jim Parkin; page 113: Shutterstock, robert paul van beets; page 114: Shutterstock, welcomia; page 116: Shutterstock, Ieva Geneviciene; page 118: Shutterstock, Arina P Habich; page 120: Shutterstock, Baloncici; page 125: Shutterstock, Steve Bower; page 126: Shutterstock, i viewfinder; page 130: Getty Images, Andy Reynolds; page 132: Shutterstock, Joseph Sohm; page 136: Shutterstock, Rob Marmion; page 137: Shutterstock, ABC Photo; page 139: Capri Camper; page 141: Shutterstock, sippakorn; page 143: Shutterstock, Baloncici; page 146: Shutterstock, ABC Photo; page 148: Shutterstock, ABC Photo; page 149: Hofmann Architecture; page 150: Shutterstock, Fetching Photos; page 152: Shutterstock: Arina P Habich; page 153: Shutterstock, ABC Photo; page 154: Shutterstock, dreamnikon; page 155: Shutterstock: Karin Hildebrand Lau; page 167: Shutterstock, JaySi; page 168: Shutterstock, Aleksey Stemmer; page 170: Shutterstock, Donald A.Katchusky; page 173: Shutterstock: Patrik Slezak; page 186: Ramie Babcock, Glamping with Boys; pages 188–191: Andreas Stavropoulos; pages 192–197: Ramie Babock; pages 198–213: Hofmann Architecture; page 224: Shutterstock,cdrin

INDEX